AUTOBIOGRAPHICAL MEMORIES

PAST – PRESENT – FUTURE

GOOD – BAD – INDIFFERENT

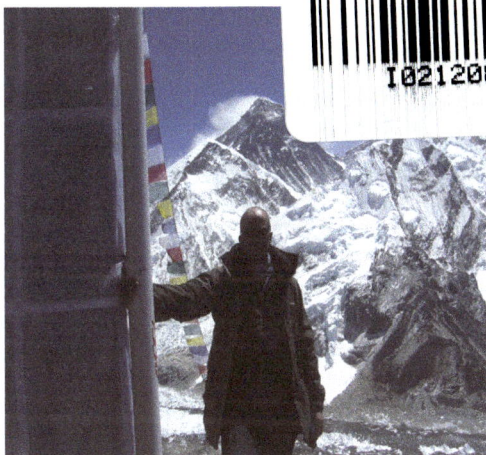

I0212086

Standing on Kalapathar 18129ft 09/04/2008,
EVEREST directly above my head

MY LIFE

(Not as a celebrity but every much as interesting)

D. L. HOROBIN-WRIGHT
Born 01/05/1961

Published by New Generation Publishing in 2013

Copyright © D. L. Horobin-Wright 2013

First Edition

The author asserts the moral right under the Copyright,
Designs and Patents Act 1988 to be identified as the author
of this work.

All Rights reserved. No part of this publication may be
reproduced, stored in a retrieval system or transmitted, in any
form or by any means without the prior consent of the
author, nor be otherwise circulated in any form of binding or
cover other than that which it is published and without a
similar condition being imposed on the subsequent
purchaser.

www.newgeneration-publishing.com

New Generation Publishing

In Loving Memory

This book is dedicated to the loving memories of both my Mum & Dad, for the love and unequivocal support they gave me and my siblings throughout life. From the circumstances as we now know them to sadly when they both left us. For myself personally I hold all that they gave me and to all that they shared with the highest esteem. I trust that in return I also gave them many happy memories to behold.

Many thanks to my wife Marion who has helped me with proof reading endlessly throughout my endeavour to write a book. The countless corrections she has had to make/suggest, especially with the words THERE & THEIR. No matter how many times it is explained to me how they fit into sentencing I still cannot grasp it. Also other close friends who have added comments for me to correct or ignore as felt necessary. At times I felt anger, however having taken on board all that has been suggested and leaving some parts in the book as they are, this is it.

Had Dr Johnson (1709-1784) written his own life, in conformity with the opinion which he has given, that every man's life may be best written by himself!

"A man (said he) who writes a book, thinks himself wiser or wittier than the rest of mankind; he supposes that he can instruct or amuse them, and the publick to whom he appeals, must, after all, be the judges of his pretensions."

CONTENTS

THE OLDER I GET – THE MORE ATTACHED TO LIFE I BECOME!

PREFACE

This is very much a personal/family book written by the second eldest son from a family of four children. Whilst it will deal with the individual's life (author) in great detail, if written correctly then the family bond/strength/unity/split should shine/show through. Its aim is to show that like many people in the world today you do not have to be a celebrity in the public eye to have lived a most fulfilling life so far and on into the future. Not only fulfilling but very interesting as well.

Unfortunately as we have become a culture that likes to claim against or sue someone some names have been altered so as not to offend.

It is hoped that this book will serve as encouragement for others to detail their own path through life and to share knowledge and wisdom as they themselves have changed. Everyone has an interpretation about life, or a book they have just read, upon revisiting this statement we could/can often change the way we say or report things. This does not make us liars, but it does elaborate on the most mundane story!! You have only to ask a politician today to understand that statement fully. If you constantly question then the mind stays healthy.

If we understand life and break people down into three types, **TURNIP – BUSINESSMAN – ARTIST**. Which one would you be? I will not explain the answer but will tell you, you can find the detailed explanation in a book called 'How To Be Happy (Though Human)'. My answer would be that I am an **ARTIST**.

At the time of starting this book I am 45 years old, not the 20 year old pop star done it, seen it type of person. No disrespect but how can you give a life story with so little to put into it. Marketing eh who would dispel it? The very machine I will need if this book ever gets released. I will endeavour to make it an interesting read and God willing my old English teacher will receive the first copy.

If this book is read carefully and you have gained/formed an opinion, read it again because it is most certain that your opinion has been addressed/answered/covered somewhere within it. Wherever possible I have tried to both provoke and answer at the same time (not always in the same chapter so beware and thoughtful).

Look for similarities, if you are around the same age as me it should serve as a reminder of events that have been long forgotten. For sure it will hopefully bring a smile to your face when you recant your long dormant memory cells!

INTRODUCTION

- **<u>Never let an excuse be the reason why you don't do it!!!!</u>**

A very warm hello to all who have bought this book, the next few paragraphs will cover why I thought I had to write such a book. Many things have influenced me throughout my life, none more important than my **MUM and DAD**.

As a child I was taught lots of sayings which I little understood, their meaning became much clearer as I journeyed through life. Some meanings were clearer quicker than others.

So why should you buy this book, or what indeed made me want to write it? Here follows a list of reasons. Some or most of you will have heard in your own life from your parents or people of influence or indeed from reading a book, lots of sayings/reasons:

- For Mum and Dad
- I am a prolific reader of books albeit mostly history and auto/biographies of (alleged) great Men and Women. The politics they suffered from in turn are no different than that in which we ourselves suffer today!
- Everyone apparently has a book in them (here is mine!)
- Thought about it for so long, now here it is whether published or not
- **<u>My life is just as interesting as others</u>**
- Make my own little piece of history
- Annotate that my life is just as interesting as any celebrity, in many cases better
- A deeply cathartic process

Upon reading please bear in mind that my thought processes are different now from when I was living through some of the periods in my life that I am talking about. Hopefully now, through age, the story will be told with more eloquence and as true to remembrance as possible. Marketing was mentioned in the Preface as a process to sell a book; it will not contain a ploy of promising sex and violence to sell it. However if you read on it will contain reference towards both, not to sell but to use in the story as necessary.

You see although we read about celebrities often in the papers or as seen on TV, we not in the public eye also live life with great or greater similarities. It is not unique to them although some would let you believe that. We feed this constant machine and they feed off it, my point would be to live your own life and enjoy in the same way for what it is and what it gives to you. Not gonna (poor English I know) become an agony aunt but as my Dad used to say **you only live once so live every day as though it's your last**. More importantly enjoy it whilst you're doing it. And this from a man who was full time disabled for the last 40 years of his life. One other saying which will be repeated in this book is "**Every day is a good day if you wake up alive**", another one of Dad's favourite sayings.

Armed with all the above and more to come, life should be enjoyable and more importantly manageable. So hopefully I now have enough of your attention for you to at least want to read more. If that is the case I sincerely hope that you find my journey exciting, funny, sad and at times fantastically good. At the very least it will make you want to read it until the end. I know that my immediate family will be interested in what I have written whether good, bad or indifferent.

I have added parts to this autobiography on an ad hoc basis whether it fits the time or explanation. My hope is that it does not detract from the story.

One point I feel the need to explain as best as I can is that before this story starts we none of us are in control of where and to whom we are born. Please do not allow the viewpoint that in today's bloody world we can now choose a sperm donor or baby, etc. What I seek to explain is that anyone born inside my first sentence has no control of the environment, country, parentage, social circumstance, etc, those who choose to have a baby through a sperm donor or adoption are a separate criteria. From what or where or to whom we are born determines who we are and what we become to a certain extent. Along with many influences that occur throughout as many years as we live. Not forgetting that people can and do change their own minds often along the journey of life. That can also mean changing a viewpoint you have held steadfast for many years even decades. Then you change your mind and alter your view, of course what's now lost is the understanding from friends, family, colleagues, etc that you can actually change your viewpoints and indeed do! Please seek from this paragraph your own understanding of its meaning and adapt as necessary throughout your lives. If it affects anyone or anything then if you can, put it right.

I also totally applaud those who choose to have a baby by other alternative methods and am appreciative that they also contribute a good upbringing for these children.

There now follows a list of people special (and some not now so special but kindly thought of!) to me whilst growing up and older, some of whom have died:

Mum & Dad, Grandma & GrandDad Lloyd, Grandma & GrandDad Horobin, Auntie Elsie & Uncle David Lapworth (not real relatives but two fantastic people), Uncle Bill, Aunt Val Lloyd & Family, Uncle Bill Barlow & Auntie Sylvia, Great Grandma Bowen, Uncle Jack, Aunt Thelma & Family, the <u>HORRIBLE HOROBIN</u> clan!!!
 Mr & Mrs Wallbank (Mrs Wallbank was like a second Mum to me), Mr & Mrs Fisher, Tony Starkey (died too young), John Barlow (also died too young), The Starkey Family, The Green Family, The Elsworth Family, Mr & Mrs Norcup and Family, Mr & Mrs Glenn & Family, Mr & Mrs Gledhill & family, The whole of the Hilltop Nuneaton Estate 1961- , Mr & Mrs Bradbury & family, Dawn Campbell, Julie Branderick, <u>MOIRA KEMSLEY</u>, The Fisher family, <u>Lol</u> & Bev & Kids (great friend), My two brothers & sister (sometimes!), Michelle Wheeler, Marion Wright, Andrea Whiteman, Jackie Shenton, Vicki, Susan Kirkbride, Gillian, Julie Silcock, Alison Glover, Rita Horton, Susannah Horstemeyer, Petra – Jasmine – Carmen, Alexander – Cat – Caitlin – Emerson, Kerry & Liberty (Granddaughter) – Charles Oddy – Barbara Griffin – Army colleagues 1980-1993
 <u>Neil & Michala – Ian & Lucy – Alex & Jill – Rachael & Phil & Boys – Tim & Allen AKA THE PIKEYS!</u>

Chapter I

CHILDHOOD AT 42 BARTON ROAD

I can safely say that unlike others I do not remember anything about my childhood from birth to about 3 to 5. Hope this does not make me a bad person but I have no enlightening thing to say about those very early still developing years. My memory does fall back to my first appreciation of our Mum and the photos will bear truth to the statement that she was beautiful. Always, to her own credit, well groomed and a credit to the efforts she made to make herself presentable on each and every occasion. So I was the second son born into our family on **1 MAY 1961**, as said previous my recollections start around 4 or 5 years old.

Dad apparently had had a few jobs whilst I was a child, the last job that I remember was that he used to work on the roads. He used to park his lorry at the bottom of our street and to a small impressionable child it was huge. Today it would not break sweat against a large Bedford van. My mind was made up I was going to become a lorry driver. Nobody told me that as I grew up my mind would develop and change, so at that time I was adamant that's what I wanted to be.

In those days the Mums were the home builders (they still are today only multi-skilled e.g. home & work) and our Mum was extremely good at it. She was very strict, something she confided later in life that she regretted. But we all told her that how she brought us up to be where we are today was testament to her. We often had jokes with her once we were older, the one that sticks out most is if she chased us down the hall if we could not jump the first 3 steps on the stairs then we were successfully hit on the bottom (I am smiling writing that statement).

Our sister (Samantha) was born on 22 September 1966, a year or so after she was born our lives were to be changed forever.

Dad went to work as usual one day and decided after his day had finished that he would help them out by doing a little more. Sadly the tractor that he was driving toppled over and crushed him, he died at the scene. Fortunately for us he was given first aid rather quickly and along with a tracheotomy (revolutionary treatment back then in 1968) started breathing again. Dad suffered brain damage which affected him all his life, don't get me wrong he was intelligent and totally corpus mentis but such was the disability it affected him in other ways. His fingers on his hands were bent over and his balance was largely affected. The best example is that if he were to fall over, by the time his brain sent the signal and said put your hands out he would have hit the floor. Subsequently over the years he could walk, albeit funnily, and he broke his nose no less than 10 times. He had a day pass at the hospital. So for the next 4 months after the accident life revolved around visiting Dad at various hospitals, for us as kids this was a great adventure. Dad did not know who we were at first and we constantly had to remind him. Do you know to this day (sadly Dad is no longer with us) I never once asked Dad how he came to accept that he knew us. I feel utterly sure that he knew we were his children but never until now sought to question it, perhaps it does not need to be questioned. Hospitals were such fun places back then, or at least that's what I thought anyway. After 4 months Mum made the biggest/bravest decision to have Dad back home again, none of us knew or understood the difficulties she faced. Dad was almost totally dependent upon our

Mum. He was a very strong and proud man but the disability must have knocked him sideways. It is testament to his strength that we were able over the next 30+ years or more to have as much fun as we did.

What we did not realise at this time was that Mum and Dad were in legal battles with the company that he worked for to obtain compensation. Sadly the only witness would not testify, my only hope is that he was comfortable with his conscience. Dare I suggest that knowing what I know now it would have been cheaper paying him off than paying Dad compensation. Even the local MP Leslie Huckfield got involved to no avail but very kind in doing so. So the case was referred to the industrial injuries board and Mum and Dad received little over £4000. They invested a £1000 for each child until each of us reached 21 years of age. My younger brother also had the same sum invested when he was born. When I became 21 with the money that I received I bought a Ford Escort with **ALLOY** wheels of which I was extremely proud and thanked my parents accordingly.

Well life revolved around Dad's attempts at rehabilitation at the hospital, I went with Dad on every visit and enjoyed it probably more than he did. Every time in the gym I got to play, maybe Dad was frustrated but for me it was nothing but joy. Like everything in life the hospitals can only do so much so Dad no longer had to go. Life with a disabled person for those that know becomes adaptable as they progress then eventually the disability regresses. Dad had always been an early bird when it came to getting out of bed. Every morning around 05:00 he got out of bed and always got me up to come downstairs and help him to get dressed. I shared a bedroom with my brothers and was the first in line when he came in so Dad always got me up. Before school each day I had already been up 4 hours before it started, something I carried out until I left home at 18. Again I was like a kid with a new toy, every morning throughout the years became a lesson. Dad, when it was light, would go for a walk with me in tow. As we walked through the fields or pathways I would get my very own nature lesson. Each bird was named, rabbit spotted, pheasants ripe for poaching shown (and how to catch them). The colours of the land and their many changes throughout the seasonal rotation, watching the world prepare itself in front of our eyes. What I found most uncanny was his ability to predict the rain or a cold day. To this very day I can do the same to almost 100% certainty, equally to this day I myself struggle to get past 04:30 asleep and am often up and about. When it was dark we would sit in the kitchen and as the day came in Dad would explain things to me. My very own teacher, it was great. One of our friends used to keep his rag and bone cart in our huge garden shed, the horse was kept in the local fields. Sometimes he allowed us to ride on it, how great that simple thing felt, wonder if kids today would find that enviable (perhaps not).

Through this period right up to adulthood Mum became a part-time Dad, as well as our actual Dad who sometimes became frustrated. Over the years our Mum was nothing short of fantastic, again we had no appreciation of how difficult life was for her as we made our ever increasing demands, not least financially. Living on disability allowance as a family of 5, soon to become 6 must have been a strain for Mum, but you would never have known. We quickly got to learn that we would rather be disciplined by Dad than Mum, because of Dad's disability he could not hit us properly. Although he made the effort it did not hurt, something we all laughed about when we became older and told them both.

When I was 11 years old my youngest brother (Alexander) was born, we were now 4 children and in a funny way Dad for Mum was the fifth. I don't mean that statement disrespectfully but Mum had to look after Dad's needs as though he were also a child. Things that Mum had to do we became aware of as we got older. But for now we were kids doing what kids do, playing and getting into the odd bit of mischief.

I must make a mention of our oldest brother and the first born son Ace, born on 4/12/1959. His name is really Arthur Charles Eric which he dislikes intensely (so sorry mate), hence the reason why we all call him A.C.E!!

I mentioned earlier words of wisdom that as a parent (and we all now are) you feel morally obligated to pass onto your children. We, I feel sure, have passed some or all of the sayings our parents passed onto us to our own children. Dad always used to say the beauty of life is the diversity of it. Massive statement that one, as a child I did not fully understand it. If one pauses and thinks about it as we know the world today it is totally APT. He also told us that even we brothers and sister are all different (not the obvious physical differences). Little did we know that throughout stages of our life we would test each other's limits in all manner of ways. Subsequently we now have a situation where we do not see or speak to our sister (more in a later chapter). What Mum and Dad did preach extensively is that no matter what the reason we fall out over is, we should work it out and move on as a family. Unfortunately with our sister this is not yet on the agenda. Obviously now as we all know a little bit about life we now know families do change, whatever influences a person or persons within it can and often do result in a family feud/split.

Sorry I digressed a little, growing up at 42 Barton Road, Hill Top, Nuneaton other than having a disabled father was pretty much normal from what I can gather when measured against other people. We became Dad's arms and legs (and remote control in the early days of television!) especially when it came to his beloved garden. I swear we were producing more vegetables than the local shop and giving it away to friends for free as they passed our fence. I built rockeries, we changed the garden eventually to lawn as we got older and left home. Mum was a big influence here and she landscaped the garden to absolute perfection. Mum really loved her garden, after all she had waited long enough over the years to get her go.

Money must have been tight throughout our schooldays but we always seemed to be ok (strong testament to our Mum here). Mum remained fantastic with money throughout her whole life.

Fond memories of the first bicycle Mum bought me from Woods Bike Shop underneath Coton Arches (long since gone). As a small child, going to Boswells (Butchers, now gone) and feeling grown up asking for a shilling's worth of dripping. My older brother always used to take the brown bit at the bottom of the pot, lovely on bread smothered in pepper. Each year the Carnival was the central attraction and the streets were packed with people (carnival floats seemed much bigger and better back then or perhaps it was because we were smaller). We all, as individuals, put pressure on Mum & Dad with our constant demands for things. I remember going mental for a pair of crepe soled platform shoes, Mum relented and bought me a pair. Instantly I disliked them, consequently I sold them to my mate Chris for 50 pence. Then the daft bugger stupidly came to our house to see if I was coming out to play. Guess what, you guessed it he was only wearing the shoes I had sold to him, Mum commented on the fact that I also had a pair just like them. To which he innocently replied "these are them", where could I hide and how fast. Not sure to this day how I got away with that one!

We had our first family holiday in Ingoldmells in a caravan when I was 12, through the social services scheme, caravans then were not like they are today. Our Mum made us wait outside whilst she cleaned it before allowing us in and I do mean thoroughly clean it. Remember the bikes at the holiday park where you could sit 3 or more abreast because they were so wide, what fun and totally new to our young eyes Today you would walk away in disgust. As a teenager Mum paid for me to go to a place called Snowdonia in Wales with my school George Eliot. Having not been out of Nuneaton much I thought it was a foreign world. The impression it left on me lasts to this day, Mount Snowdon was the first mountain I ever climbed. The journey to Snowdon was truly spectacular to my eyes, especially the tranquillity of it all (I did not know that word back then!) When I die it is my wish that my ashes are scattered from it to allow me freedom in totally beautiful surroundings. I climb in Snowdonia at least ten times each and every year. I never get bored of its tranquil beauty (thanks to Mum) and the realisation of just how insignificant we are as humans hell-bent on ruining this world of ours.

My brothers and sister would have to verify if indeed they thought that something was missing from their lives as they grew up. From my point of view I can only say that all, as far as I am concerned, was very good. I had no reason to believe otherwise and certainly as I am now a lot older than that time I still think the same. All that I have gained from life so far has been through personal endeavour and with the support of my parents.

I have always had a healthy interest in the human body, hence my First Aid achievements first with the Red Cross and latterly with St Johns Ambulance. My father had an old friend who lived along Heath End Road, Nuneaton. His name, or rather nickname, was Yanto (he was from Wales and had very broad accent), at least that's how I think it was spelt. Yanto was the local Pit First Aider for many years; he was now retired and lived with his wife. Dad arranged for me to visit him weekly to learn all about the human body. Each week I was tested on names of parts all over the body, pressure points had to be both known and shown; his good lady also provided home baked cakes (fantastic cook). They were and still are in my memory blissful moments in my life, Yanto was very keen and strict in his teaching. I was there to learn and not waste his time, sadly they are both no longer with us but I remember them fondly. Also around this time I became involved with the Red Cross and later in life St John's. Now I got to practice bandages and splints each week. During my time within the Red Cross movement we had occasion to work with children with disabilities, today they would be called Learning Disabilities. But back then they were Spastic, Mongol, etc, not nice terms I agree but that was the way it was then. In this I revelled, looking after these people was a revelation in itself; sadly some of them were terminally ill and died. I distinctly remember a young lad called David; he was only 11 years old and dying. In fact he died not long after I met him but his ability to be just like any other child growing up knew no bounds. Full of fun and mischief, I'm not sure if he knew he was going to die (I suspect not). Susan was another who also lived along Heath End Road, she took a shine to me when I worked at Horsley, Smith & Jewson at the end of Heath End Road on a Saturday. On the way to work I passed her house, she ran out to greet me every time. I have worked with various organisations over the years looking after people. Brent Council in London utilised my skills (aged 36), we took the kids and adults into Wormwood Scrubs prison to be chaperoned by people serving life sentences. Take away the reason why these people were in prison, they knew these kids inside out and the joy was reciprocal. As soon as the kids entered the room they went straight to the lags with whom they had built up a personal and close relationship. Although mentally they were never going to survive in society as we know it, they were at ease with each respective person they met and worked with.

A massive mention must now go to a few people who were not just family friends but who also assisted me in my growing up process. Mum had a friend we called Auntie Elsie, her husband we called Uncle David. They were not related to us at all and they were much older than Mum. I loved them both as a couple and individuals, Auntie Elsie used to ask us to run errands for her. She was a bit of a rebel as well; at the time I was trying to become a smoker. Often I used to accompany her on her weekly visit to the club where she used to let me have a lager shandy! Mum would have gone mad but Auntie Elsie also used to let me smoke a cigarette from time to time, I felt like an adult, almost. Uncle David could not read or write, sadly after Auntie Elsie died we had to read and reply to all his letters. The love and affection between us all was fantastic, again I am smiling just thinking about them both. We looked after him until he passed away, in fact it was my younger brother who found him dead in his chair. He loved it when we became old enough to have a pint with him and more importantly could drive him to the pub. Both will never be forgotten. Other families known on the estate, Arnold, Born, Bradbury X2, Bradford, Brown, Bird, Cypryk, Deakin, Devlin, Elsworth, Evans, Fisher, Gledhill, Green, Hood, Holland, Hall, Harrison X2, Handley, Harvey, Harper, Ireland, Irish Family, Jones X2, Kirkbride, Leadbeater, LeBlanq, Lapworth, Norcup, Nash, Porter, Parker, Big Pete, Proctor, Quinton, Riley, Starkey, Shepherd, Turner, Varden, White, Weller, Woods, Wallbank, Tom & Wendy, Clay, York, Duffy, Millerchip , Bayliss, note just how many people we knew, equally about half again whose surnames escape me at the moment (today most people do not even know their neighbours, **SAD**) etc all helped form my teenage years and gave me a lot of tellings off as well. Mrs Wallbank sadly lost her husband to an accident outside the Wharfe Inn. I loved this lady just like a mother, in fact I used to tell her and my Mum that she was my second Mum. No one would or did dare to treat this woman like a fool. She coped magnificently with a large family after her husband was killed. She had love enough for all, her parties were a joy to attend for all kids, the like of which we will never see again. Every bonfire night became a huge party on her garden with bonfire, fireworks and lots of food. As her children grew up they used to put on parties in the house, the girls used to dress up, sing and act. Again a lady I will never forget, nor any member of her family. Her son Eddie and I became great friends as we grew up together on the estate.

Steam trains were another source of fascination back in those days, every time we heard one all the kids on the estate would run down the hill to the bridge over the railway line. Stand on it (stupidly) to be covered in steam from the engine; it truly seemed fun at the time.

Looking back though I feel sure this was a dangerous thing to do.

Always as kids we were keen to play football, although unlike today not every child actually owned one. Any kid who had a football instantly became a popular friend to have. Not forgetting of course that we are old enough to remember the leather footballs with the bladder inside. How heavy did those balls become when it rained or became wet? Well naturally we had energy to burn and neighbours windows to break as we went for that extra special goal or power kick. There was always a neighbour who would not let you have the ball back, they would either not give you the ball at all or waited until they had first spoken to your parents. We even had a match each year between Hill Top and Bermuda Village and not forgetting against parents each and every summer in the fields. Well as the years passed, aged 16 I was asked to go and train with a local football team called Hill Top Sports who were one of the top local sides of the day. It opened up a new world for me, at first I was overawed by it all but quickly settled into playing for one of the reserve teams. It was not long before I progressed to playing for the first team; over the years I have been told that I have a good engine (but would have been better served if I had taken the ball with me more often!). I have played for the following teams over the years:

- Hill Top Sports
- Donnithorne (winning the local league and cup)
- Huntingdon Sports (York)
- Various Army Teams (winning the local league)
- Zum Stadtholz (Local German team winning many trophies and tournaments)

- Fortuna Moenchengladbach (semi – pro) West Germany
- Waldniel (Semi – pro) West Germany
- Elliot & Star (London top Amateur Team)

I have also played football at Bayer Uerdingen Stadium and the Berlin Olympic Stadium and had trials for the Army divisional team in West Germany. Sadly though, my playing career ended in April 2001 aged 39 during a five a side tournament. In a rather innocuous tackle at the end of the last game during the final I snapped my right leg just above the ankle. Completely breaking both bones (the pain I can assure you was horrendous). Since that day I have had a further 3 operations on the leg to remove pins and scar tissue damage. The leg is not 100% straight but it is as good as it is ever going to be.

My thoughts right now go back to games we played along with antics we got up to as teenagers, as passed down I assume from the older boys. Have a read, for some it will jog a long forgotten memory. For the youth of today they will probably find it too tame, they prefer to drink beer and fight in gangs, which is so sad. If only we could get through to the young at an earlier age that you only have one opportunity in this life. Grab it with as much energy as you can. Anyway back to the games along with a simple explanation:

- Hedgehopping, either along the front of gardens or around the back. Trouble with around the back was that as you jumped you never knew what was on the other side of the hedge/fence; you could and did break glass (small glass plant beds!) best played at night!

- Talio, a game whereby 1 person was the catcher and the others had to hide and not get caught. Once caught the catcher had to chase and hold you and say Talio 1-2-3 and then you had to help him or her to catch the rest. Problem here was who stuck to the boundaries, often getting caught in someone's garden by the owner/s. Some games ended when people who had to be in for a certain time went home and left you all alone still hiding or searching.

- Walking across the railway bridge parapet in order to get covered in steam from the steam train (remember them). Talk about dangerous.

- Putting detonators on the rail track to stop a train, remember the little sheds at the side of the track they used to keep them in, thankfully they are all gone now and they carry the detonators on the trains under lock and key.

- Constantly phoning the signalman up on the track side phone

- Balance cans on the rail track and knock them off with stones **(Please stay off railways they are dangerous)**

- Gathering the grass cuttings from the field and using them to land on whilst doing somersaults from the slide.

- Swinging and seeing how far you could jump forward from a swing. The brave carried out a 360 degree turn. You have to see it to believe it.

- Winter-Warmers, remember when winter really was a cold affair. We used to get an empty paint can (made of tin back then), knock holes into it. Tie wire through the top as a handle; fill it with wood and coal. Obviously light it and walk around the streets or the fields and swing it through the air allowing the oxygen to feed the fire. Big flames, warm hands, job done. Today it would be banned for sure; if you were ambidextrous you could swing one with each arm.

- Door knocking, a firm favourite this one, every bonfire night it became banger door knocking. God we were rebels

- Using a straight bicycle handlebar as a gun. Leave the rubber on one end, place the banger in the other and shoot it. **(PLEASE DO NOT REPEAT THIS OR ANYTHING ABOVE, NOT EVEN FOR NOSATLGIA)**

- Catapults, come on the memories are now in full swing, constant target practice using cans on a wall

- Arrows, collecting suitable wood, skin it, smooth it, sharpen the point, split the top end and place the flights in. Usually the flights were made from a cereal packet. A length of string with a knot in one end. Loop the string over the knot at the pointed end and hold the length of rope along the shaft length. Then with all your might pull your arm back and launch it high and long - hopefully

- Collecting spider webs, you hardly see any at all these days unless you're really in the country. Easy to do, collect a very thin branch from a bush, take the leaves off, make a circle and cross the two ends, tie off and place under each web and gently lift off. (Not a practice you should carry out today you understand)

- Collecting birds eggs, again very much today **a NO, NO, NEVER**

- Cowboys and Indians, why was I always on the losing side?

- Family fun days as set up by all the parents every summer, they really used to take over in the summer and challenge all the kids. It was great being able to beat them if we could and often did (maybe that was the plan). Community spirit was really great back then. Total applause to all those who still make the effort today and to all those that don't, come on do it.
- Paper/Scissors/Rock
- Conkers, lots of painful misses along with it wrapping around yourself, remember soaking them in vinegar and baking them in the oven. Who owned a conker that had won 100 matches (I did!) called a laggy I believe
- Collecting bull rushes to sell to people in the summer to decorate homes
- Derelict houses to explore (what fun and scary too)
- Taking back empty beer/pop bottles to claim the refund
- Milk tokens from doorsteps back to the Co-Op for a refund
- Sprinting past the local fruit shop and taking an apple or pear from the display outside - I don't nor have I ever eaten fruit so why!
- Swimming in the local lagoon, lake or canal as well as diving from the cliffs
- Building endless camps and hides in the fields
- Lying down on your back looking up into the bright clear sky at night and dreaming or putting the world to rights
- Kerb(ie), 2 players on opposite sides of the road. The aim is to throw the ball and hit the kerb opposite to score 1 point, 2 points if it bounces off the kerb and you catch it. Each time you miss

your opponent gets a go to achieve a pre-determined score to win the game.

- Hit the ball against the wall or anything that is solid. The aim is to have lots of players and define the boundaries. You each kick the ball one at a time in order to hit the wall (in boundary), if you miss you drop out until a winner is found.

- Always squeezing that extra 10 mins + out of playing out, before your parents went mad

- Poaching: although we had a lot of fun we were forever catching rabbits to sell on the estate (Mums could skin and gut rabbits in them days). We also used to catch pheasants by putting a net up over the hedgerows and chasing them into it. Not to be recommended today I may add, it seemed ok at the time and everyone was doing it if they could.

- Borrowing coal (for permanent use) from the opencast coalmine until it closed, often people got caught!

- Chopping wood to sell as firewood (always a good earner until someone started it as a business)

- Rope swing: Brilliant fun, find a large tree, hang a thick (preferably) rope from it and swing. Then it gets more complicated, how many people can swing on one rope. Why did I always seem to be on the bottom when it snapped? Which it often did. Let's hang a rope from a tree over a brook or canal and then, you guessed it, someone gets wet. The fun from this was endless and dangerous at times.

- Marbles, winning preferably but if you lost endlessly trying to rearrange a rematch to win them back. Not forgetting the stunnies (ball bearings). Constantly changing the rules so you would not lose the game

- Climbing street lamp posts, spit on your hands and climb to the top, if you could get to the top on one dose of spit on your hands you were special (please don't try this)
- Scrumping for apples even though I don't like or eat fruit at all
- Fossil hunting for Ammonites, along the edge of the railway used to be the place to find them under stones
- Turning up stones to find slow worms

Scars & Injuries from Childhood to Adulthood through Accidents/Sport/Assault:

1. Right leg (thigh) barbed wire aged 5
2. Right wrist (window trying to attract someone's attention) aged 12/13
3. Right big toe (garden fork) aged 12/13
4. Left hand palm (splinter from palm to full length of finger) fence aged 13/14
5. Left front temple (golf club) aged 13/14
6. Right index front of finger (machine cutter) aged 18
7. Dislocated both thumbs from childhood to adulthood (irregular intervals)
8. Right hand palm (discharged cartridge) Army manoeuvres aged 21
9. Left Pectoral scar due to falling over my bed (drunk) aged 22
10. Dislocated right elbow (showing off backward flick flak) aged 25
11. Left shoulder (dislocation) playing rugby aged 26

12. Right inside forearm before elbow (fell through a roof off a brickyard chimney ladder) drunk aged 26
13. Head L/H/Side (football, I was heading the ball as he kicked me!) aged 29
14. Right shoulder (dislocation) bobsleighing aged 30
15. Behind left ear (assault, glassed) aged 38
16. Right leg (both bones broken above the ankle) football aged 39
17. Right knee (scar tissue as a result of the above) aged 42/43
18. Upper lip R/H/side (boating, windlass through lip) aged 46

I have to admit to being fed up with having accidents now, surely I am far too old and wise to have them. How can I teach anyone younger than myself how to be careful when I cannot afford the same luxury to myself? If we have a god and he/she is listening can we please stop now as I really have had enough, thanks.

Memory lane of jobs to assist Mum in her daily work/chores:

- Rinsing the clothing using a mangle, turning the handle as fast as I could to catch my brother's fingers in it if he was not careful
- Carrying the shopping from town to home (approx 1 mile), could not afford bus/taxi and did not have a car
- Sweeping the street in front of your house (not much of that today)
- Making bottle feed for my younger brother (I ate more Farley's Rusk than he got I can assure you)

- Fetching a 56lb bag of potatoes as a teenager from the local farm carrying it on my shoulders for .7 mile, potatoes cheaper than local shops and lasted longer
- Blackberry picking, a battle with other kids to pick the most so that your Mum could bake a pie
- Hoovering at weekends, often for pocket money
- Gardening from youth to adulthood
- Cleaning windows with Windolene (smudges galore!)
- Walking with Dad in case he fell (he fell often sadly)

Money making ventures as a child to teenager:

- Paper round (great for me being an early riser)
- Chopping and selling firewood
- Taking back beer bottles to the off licence of each pub for a penny per bottle
- Selling bullrushes picked from the local clayhole
- Gardening for older folk
- Digging trenches for the pipeline layers for pocket money
- Collecting/borrowing! milk tokens and taking them back to the Co-Op for the money

Things you will never see or hope to experience:

- Outside toilets along with the obligatory spiders, very cold places especially in the winter. Paint flaking off the walls no matter how many times they were painted.

- Water tanks outside above coalhouse and toilet
- Newspaper actually being used as toilet paper, many families could not afford the real thing.
- Remember the public toilet loo paper, clear and as smooth as glass. Did it wipe or spread? We used to pinch it and use it as tracing paper!
- TVs without remote control (black and white)
- Making Christmas decorations from material, to be hung all over the rooms
- Cables plugged into sockets using matchsticks
- Using inside cigarette packets silver foil to make fuses
- Coalhouse or coal bunkers
- Rag and bone man (horse and cart), might be some left somewhere
- Steam trains
- Red phone boxes (nearly all gone now)
- Cigarettes and chewing gum sold in machines on street walls by shops
- Pre-Decimal coins
- Record players with bale arms
- 33/45rpm records
- Walkmans

A famous picture of myself watering the RHUBARB from my very own unique watering system!! Always brought out on visits and discussed. Aged 6/7 1967/8

Our beloved dog, LASSIE, in the back garden. The shed in the background was loaned to a friend for his rag and bone cart

My older brother Ace and me (Dean) Check out the
BOB haircut, a fashion trend ahead of its time

Ace – Samantha – Alexander - Dean

Family complete

Mum – Dad – Ace – Dean – Samantha - Alexander

Chapter II

SCHOOLDAYS

We lived on a council estate in Nuneaton called Hill Top, the reason I say that is because it seemed at the time as though we were different from the other kids that came from the big private estates. Of course we know now that there is no difference, unless of course you are from the rich who deem it their responsibility to make us pay for them to become richer and they truly think they are different. My suggestion here is to read history (a favourite subject of mine) books and work out the answer for yourself **(National Trust!)**

Sorry I digressed this chapter is about school, well just because Dad was disabled did not mean that we could not go to school. Mum made our school life as exciting as it could be and our lives were very rich because of her. As Mum almost took over from Dad all discipline matters were carried out by her, especially where school was concerned. We were not as well off as other kids but we were rich in other ways not least in the love that we were given by Mum.

My first school was Chilvers Coton (demolished now), from memory my start to school life was most enjoyable. Learning at the beginning was, to my memory, very enjoyable. Picking up things rather quickly I shot through reading books like a true professional. I love reading to this day and have amassed quite a collection of books in our library at home. Quite why or where I lost interest later in life is beyond explanation. I remember with a passion each year getting ready for harvest festival and taking in a donation of food to the church for people less well off. Such an exciting time to celebrate the harvest, it is my single most lasting early memory. To fill up and decorate your box before delivery was an absolute joy. It all seemed to run like clockwork from the time we started the day until the end. It probably gave Mum a well earned break as well from demanding children. Learning to read and write was equally enjoyable, proudly taking home the little books to read to Mum and Dad.

I then went to Middlemarch Junior School; suddenly it got tougher as the teachers were trying to prepare us for this big world of ours. Lessons got harder, English, maths, etc. Still I buckled down and tried my best but was often too easily distracted, something I suffered from a lot during school life. Too easily led I believe they call it, still life was good and school was a necessary occupation. One lasting observation, and having spoken to other people like me who are left handed, the teachers would often take the pen or pencil from my left hand and place it into my right. I have shared this with other left handed people who like me have no understanding as to why they did it.

I remember vividly the playground attendant Mrs White. A strict but truly wonderful lady, it was certainly what I needed. One day whilst telling me off she held my wrist so tight that I could not get away, she was strong. We often shared a laugh as I became an adult and chatted to her as she lived near our house. Sadly one of the best ones is no longer with us. Hope to talk to her again when it is my time to leave this earth.

What was prevalent in schools of that period, and still is today, is that some children take it upon themselves to tease others. Now apparently I have a quick, hot temper (who me?), because Dad was different they used to say your Dad is a spastic or spaz for short. Well the fights and arguments I used to get into on that statement alone would be too numerous to mention. The father of one boy came to our house one evening, I had hit his son because he would not stop calling my Dad names. I had already explained to my Mum what had happened. He told my Mum that if she did not hit me then he would. I saw a side to my Mum that day that I previously didn't know existed. Had he not gone away after Mum gave him a piece of her mind I remain convinced that he would have come to harm.

Back to school, looking back I guess I had bouts of determination mixed in with asking 'what am I doing here?' Did I apply myself enough? The answer is probably no. But whatever they instilled in me, whether I showed them the results there and then or not has stood me in good stead ever since. I fondly look back and think of the lesson structures I was taught and have used them in my studies over the years. We all had favourite teachers and looking back at the old school reports Mum kept, what they said was true, good when applying himself but cares little if not pushed. Too easily distracted that's my problem, along with good old peer pressure.

Still school was good because sport was high on the agenda, the reason for that stood me in good stead especially in Chapter IV (ARMY). I loved sport and because we did not have the distractions we have in today's world I was always out playing, running or at the Nuneaton Boys Boxing Club. Little did I know how strong I was to become later in life and for what sport or purpose.

Well as for all school children what we little realised was how governments worked and that due to rule changes it meant schools could become more selective on who they allowed to attend. Subsequently a very good school I attended for 1 year suddenly became unavailable. The school is worthy of naming, Arbury High School (now St Thomas Moore). I had to move to a school which was not very well thought of (George Eliot), along with other pupils we had no choice but to conform. Mum always said it was the reason why my performance dropped. Today however I have turned out alright as I will explain in another chapter. So to the new school I fell into line and became a victim of peer pressure. I thought it was big to belong but it is not I can assure you of that. Subsequently my collar was felt by the police twice, each time I was fined by the courts and grounded by Mum. Trust me I feared Mum more than anything ever since.

As I approached my 14th birthday I started to get turned on by page 3 of the Sun newspaper (adolescents eat your heart out). Girls were suddenly more interesting, although my attempts with girlfriends thereafter were comedic to say the least. How many times must one get slapped before you understand NO means NO? Still I was hell bent on finding out what this sexual preoccupation was all about. Masturbation came into my life, living in a house with three other siblings was difficult but I managed it with the help of various page 3 women. Thoughts then turned to actual sex. I was now 14 and a man (yeah right!), no sex education in our house though. I remember Dad telling me a few years later that I should wear a condom. So here I was, this hormonal 14 year old ready for sex (or was I?). Please allow me to state that I do not think that at 14, I or anyone should have explored this issue, but I did. I believe sex education is more to the fore today than when I was at school. Anyway I met a girl (D) and she was already sexually active, wow all my dreams had come true. We were invited to a party at a friend's house, his parents were obviously more liberal than mine because they allowed him to have a party! What's more his parents were not there! Anyway me and D found our way to a bedroom. D had brought some condoms and, having instantly gained the obligatory erection (within 10 milliseconds!) D placed a condom on my penis. After some heavy petting D climbed on top of me and started moving, after approximately 60 seconds (being generous) I had an orgasm. For years afterwards I thought that 60 seconds was enough, nobody told me I had to pleasure her as well. Boy did I have some catching up to do on that score. School was great after all.

Next I moved into examination territory and can say that I did not do myself justice at that time, despite the best efforts from the school itself and my Mum. Both Mum and Dad have encouraged us in all our endeavours to make a living throughout our lives. This was also the time that Careers teachers came into the school curriculum. Fantastic, they now employed people to tell you how good, or bad, you would do or become throughout life. Did they not have the foresight to realise that people actually do change? After what was really examination failure, except for **English** and **Woodwork CSEs,** I had an interview with the Careers teacher. I was very politely told that I had almost wasted my entire school career and that I would be lucky to be employed. I was one of the few people who actually left school at 16 who had a job to go to the day that I left and I have been in continuous employment ever since, Earlier I mentioned that I remembered my lessons and caught up academically in life as I moved through it. What I was taught then but did not always listen to I apply today, since I left school I have gained the following qualifications:

- City & Guilds Engineering Technology Level 1-2-3
- City & Guilds Electrical Engineering Level 1-2-3

- City & Guilds Numeracy
- City & Guilds Communications Skills
- City & Guilds Information Technology
- City & Guilds Business Administration
- Associate Member of the Institute of Training & Development
- Underground Ticketing Systems maintenance
- Fitness Instruction & Gymnasium management
- Children's Football Coach F.A.
- A.B.A. Boxing Coach
- HGV 2 / Forklift / Motorbike
- Industrial Training Society management level 3
- Customer Services Technical Trainer (currently trainer for a global company for revenue collection systems)
- RSA German Language Basic & German speaking & Listening Level 3
- Football Leaders (children)
- Holistic/Therapeutic Body massage
- St John First Aid Instructor
- 7303 Teacher Training Course **PTLLS 2010**

Currently studying German Language and Piano as well as reading for a future History course.

Favourite TV Programmes growing up from black and white to colour:

Abbot & Costello
Benny Hill
Bless this House
Blue Peter
Bonanza
Butterflies
Casey Jones & the Cannonball Express

Carry on Films
Dick Emery
Dixon of Dock Green
Hawaii Five O
Kenny Everett Show
Keystone Cops
Larry Grayson
Laurel & Hardy
Les Dawson
Love thy Neighbour
Magpie
Magic Roundabout
Morecambe & Wise
On the Buses
Poldark
Rising Damp
Royal Variety
Saturday Night at the London Palladium
Starsky & Hutch
Steptoe & Son
Swapshop
Wheeltappers & Shunters Club
Z-Cars

With my great mate Eddie Wallbank whose family I was close to whilst growing up. I used to call his Mum my second Mum

I loved that jumper! Aged approx 12/13

Check out the trousers, how many buttons?!

This believe it or not was at the front of our house, not with my girlfriend but with my Mum

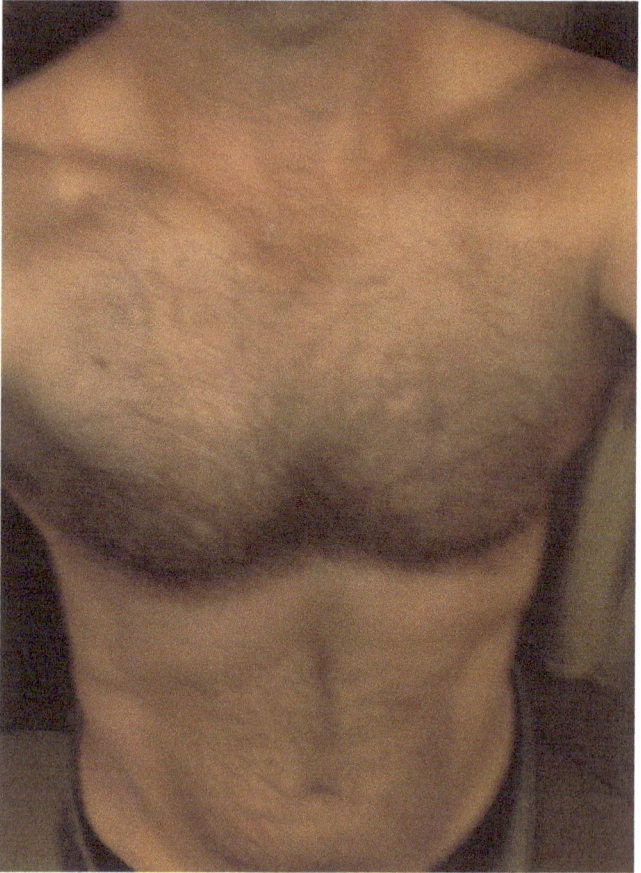

Dean (Aged 48)

Chapter III

WORKING LIFE

At the tender age of 16 I left school and embarked on the big wide world of work, armed with my CSEs in English and woodwork. With these two qualifications I applied for anything and everything, sometimes I got a reply but more often than not I did not hear anything. I may add that these applications were made in abundance before I actually left school. Also note that whilst qualifications were a very good thing in those days they were not always necessary to obtain a job, unlike in today's world.

My Uncle Henry was a manager at the Co-Op dairy and I believe my Dad may have asked him to take a look at me. So I was employed as a milkman from the day that I left school. Early starts (perfect for me) meant early finishes, except at the weekends which were collection (money) days. My wage was the princely sum of £19 per week after tax, this I handed over to Mum and she would give me pocket money to spend, saving £5 for me each week. I was rich beyond my wildest dreams and every Friday bought two packets of Maltesers and all my favourite comics, going straight upstairs for some privacy in our shared bedroom to read them. Now you hear a lot of stories about milkmen and activities of a sexual nature. The only memorable thing that happened to me was upon collecting money from a house on the round the daughter came to the door to pay (about 16-18). She had her dressing gown on, upon giving me the money her robe came open and exposed a beautiful naked body. She ran off all embarrassed, her Mum came and apologised and it took all my strength not say 'what for?' However rumours about my colleagues were widespread, that's all I can say.

After almost two years as a milkman I left and joined a foundry (Dunns) which paid me £35 a week (even richer). Dunn's was sub-contracted work by the Ford motor company, mainly manifolds were built here. I worked my socks of doing piecework each weekend and some weeks took home upwards of £70. Sadly I got into trouble at work with a colleague, we clocked off work early to fight each other. It does not matter that I won the fight outside of work as I subsequently lost my job. The issue I have is that in the fight I lost total control and badly injured the person concerned. Not, repeat not, something in reflection that I am proud of. Had I been a true man I would have just walked away.

The only good thing to come out of all this is that shortly after this incident I joined the Army and embarked on a fantastic 13 year career which changed me in many ways. You need to read the next chapter which explains my Army career in great detail.

A shortish chapter I know, fortunately I've not had many jobs. Other job roles I undertook albeit briefly were:

- Storeman as a civilian for the Army
- First Aid Instructor (St Johns, Baker St, London)
- Cadogan Tate (furniture removals)
- CUBIC 1994 to date

Chapter IV

THE ARMED FORCES 1980 – 1993

Graham Patrick Lambie 2IDSR York – M 196
Gary Green 4ADSR Herford – M 193
David Robert Howes 4ADSR Herford – M 196

The three names mentioned above are worthy of being at the head of this chapter due to the fact that they all very sadly lost their lives whilst serving as soldiers. I remember them regularly and always say a silent prayer for them and their families and will do so until the day that I myself die. They were each great and lovely people that I had the good fortune to meet and spend time with. We indeed remember and offer a toast to them at our 5 yearly interval reunions, the next one (30 years) being in **Newcastle** at St James Park on the **First Weekend of June 2015 @ 1200hrs**. Their memory is intact and displayed at the Arboretum in Alrewas, shown on the walls next to each name.

On a winters day in November 1980 having been successful in trials and tests at Sutton Coldfield I arrived in Darlington to join the Army. Allow me to explain how the Army came about, having lost my job (fighting, that temper again) I was forced to look for other work. My older brother Ace was already serving in Germany in the Royal Corps of Signals. He told me many stories which lit my eyes up, bar the ones about BASIC training which I will explain in a while. At Sutton Coldfield my intention was to join the R.E.M.E. (Royal Electrical Mechanical Engineers) (Our Dad served with the R.E.M.E. during his National Service, see photo of Dad later in this book on top of a

Scammell aged 18) however job allocation for that corps was closed. They ascertained that I had a serving brother already so I was dispatched to the Royal Corps of Signals. I was 19 and a full half when I joined the Army.

We were met at Darlington (Nov 1980) by two regular soldiers who greeted us (there were others on the train like me, new recruits) with more than a few expletives (was this allowed?), they just kept shouting! They kept this up for almost the whole 11 weeks, throughout the length of basic training. From Darlington we got on an Army bus (very slow and cold) and drove to Catterick Garrison, off the bus into the barracks (11 Signal Regiment) and the shouting really took off once again. Well, what had I let myself in for?!

Apparently from day one they seek to form you into a fighting soldier/unit by first stripping you bare (not naked) and rebuilding you as an efficient very professional soldier/person. This took many forms and you would be amazed at exactly just how much fun we had throughout it. I feel sure that others who would tell this story may have a differing opinion of it. Well where do we start? Check this list out:

- Haircut (very short)
- Moustaches if fully grown or permission given by the Army to grow one (not in training though)
- Accommodation, very clean and we were responsible for its upkeep
- Barracks, responsible for keeping it clean as well
- Other troops at varying stages of training (lots of rivalry)

- Develop and learn new skills, soldiering/fieldcraft/first aid/weapons/map reading/military law/drill/fitness etc never ending
- Development of pride, both in you the person and the Corps that you joined
- If you fail the 11 week course you are attached to another troop and start again (please not me)
- Late nights and even earlier mornings (sometimes only 2 hours sleep - **FACT**)
- Receiving information that you will never in a lifetime ever forget, the easiest is your service number (**24584113**)

Talk about being green, my brother had told me nothing about these happenings only stories of being a regular fully trained soldier. The next 11 weeks were going to be a joy – **NOT**!

My full opinion of basic training, which is what I will share with you now came about after passing out and becoming a regular fully trained soldier. Whilst going through the 11 weeks, along with my new found colleagues it was most certainly tough. The testing of both individual and collective personnel was very demanding and I saw grown adults cry and some of them leave the Army. The thought processes of myself and others were largely pushed to one side whilst developing the thought processes of becoming a soldier. Meeting up with colleagues in later years we did, and were able to, look back on basic training not only with affection but as character building for each and every one of us. We were not cloned but by the very definition of the training syllabus we had and were becoming soldiers of the highest professional nature.

I have deliberately kept basic training simple to read and would hope that your picture of it is gained from all that I have described above. With exception of the following points, which are personal to me and hopefully a little funny. Fitness was always my main strong point as an individual. I was ready-made to suit the rigorous training that the Army put you through. I later in my career became an Army Physical Training Instructor. Being fit also backfired at times as it has been documented that I cruised through various courses on the fitness front (it was true but I never admitted it to them). I will tell you more about where my physical strengths took me to later in this book. You meet some right characters in the Army, despite the hard time they were giving us we had some great laughs along the way. Every day there is an inspection of some kind, your room, cleanliness, equipment and clothing. All Army clothing had to be folded and measured before putting it into the lockers. All rooms to be clean and linen baskets to be clean and empty especially on inspection. Well one day we were inspected and they found a dirty pair of underpants in a colleague's linen basket. They sent him outside to collect two dustbins; upon his return they called us all out into the corridor. They made him stand in one of the dustbins whilst placing the second one over his head (they were both full with rubbish), proudly stating that if anyone wanted to be a grot then they can live like one. He was there for the next hour before he was told to take them away and clean up along with a loss of privileges for the next month. In my own room (3 people in it) they inspected, before they inspected they asked the person nearest the window to open the large sash window. We were on the first floor, luckily my locker passed the inspection but the guy next to me failed. They pushed his locker (double wardrobe size) through the window. The look of abject horror on our faces would have made a great picture, but we had to keep quiet. He too lost his privileges and had to fetch and repair his locker and clothing. Two short stories, but both very true. They did not, repeat did not, break our resolve to get through it, whilst enduring it it was sometimes hard. We did collectively however have a lot of fun and broke many rules for which we were never caught (but they knew we were doing it because they did it before us in their own training).

The end of the 11 weeks culminates in a passing out parade which all families are invited to. A wonderful day out to see sons/husbands/friends complete all they had learned. The preparation for this day alone was immense, constantly polishing boots to be shiny on the toe caps, pressing uniforms over and over again. They meet the Instructors and staff whom we all talk highly of even if they did piss us off at times. Our parade suffered from a massive downpour of snow which resulted in us not being seen at all by our families when marching around the parade square. However the occasion was so rewarding that no one bothered about it at all. We were now fully trained soldiers and were extremely proud of the fact. Two weeks holiday now before we returned to Catterick to our Trade Training School to train in a subject we had already chosen as a career. I was to become an Electrician Driver. God did we now think we were special, in the Trade Training School as fully fledged soldiers. How we did laugh at the unfortunate new recruits whenever we had occasion to see them (done our bit you see, basic training's not tough at all, yeah right!!). Trade training lasted for 6 weeks where we were taught how to maintain and repair generators for telecommunications both on vehicles and on their own trailers. The generators were all sizes from 300kw to 27.5KVA 3 phase. The joys of mathematics when deciding the size of generator to take on manoeuvres, ohms law used extensively in calculating wattage and amperage capacities.

The Army is a very competitive world; if you have drive and you want to excel in all that you do. My strength as I said earlier was my fitness which remained throughout my 13 years of service. Towards the end of trade training talk is uppermost of your first posting and of where you will go to serve your first tour. You have an interview where you are told about the locations of service. Again they asked if I had a relative in the forces so I told them about my brother who was by then serving in Germany. I was posted to the same regiment which I thought was rather nice. I had never before left the country or even flown on an aeroplane, here I was about to achieve both.

In May 1981 aged 20 I arrived at RAF Gutersloh to be met by a corporal from my new regiment in Bunde. He was a nice bloke who allayed all my fears and made me feel most welcome. I met my brother at the regiment and 2 hours later was posted out to a squadron of the same regiment 12 miles away in Lubbecke. Hello brother, goodbye for now brother. Off I went to my new squadron arriving at night time with no one around, that night I walked into the local town. I fell in love with Germany very early on, I spent 11 of my 13 years in the country and have been back to visit many times since that first day.

So now at my first regiment as the new boy and did they let me know it, lots of duties, all the rubbish (sh*t) jobs. Off to the stores for a long wait, spirit level bubble, etc. Guess they thought it was funny, looking back I suppose it was although during it you wondered when it was going to end. As in everything we do throughout life you have to give, as well as earn respect. I mentioned earlier that my fitness was above average and this quickly helped me in my early career. Throughout all the mandatory physical tests, as well as at sports days, I quickly shone through. Subsequently I was selected for many races along with other challenges (something I still do to this day, although a little bit slower). Also being sporty meant spending a lot of time in a tracksuit, training and competing, something that later in my career I managed to do fulltime. I competed for each Regiment, The Army & Combined Services. I have a passion for boxing and had spent time as a schoolboy learning the trade at Nuneaton Boy's Club. I must mention my trainer Dennis Panter, a lovely, very strict man who is sadly no longer with us. All who met him will never forget him. Well in the Army boxing is massive, so I was thrust into the team, knocking everyone over until I reached the final at Bunde in 1981. This was the Regimental Novice Grade 3 final at Middleweight. Anyway the fights are over three 2 minute rounds. I knocked my opponent down twice in round one for a mandatory count of 8 each time. To his credit he got back up and carried on until the end of round three. Everyone was chanting my name (Deano) which I enjoyed hearing throughout my boxing career. At the end of round three I went back to my corner jubilant, surely awaiting the judge's announcement that I had won. Everyone else was convinced I had won. When they gave the decision and raised his hand I was most upset. How could they get it so wrong I thought? Having progressed through a variety of sports I can only summise that bad decisions are made along the way with other politics. We have all at some stage in our lives watched events and been amazed at the eventual winner. Anyway suffice to say that this really fired me up to win it the next year. I never met the same opponent again, he sadly retired apparently. I carried on boxing for the next 5 years as well as competing in other sports (mention them later).

I was posted to York in England in 1982 as the regiment was moved back to the UK. There I won the boxing final in 1983 against a very tough opponent (Dickie Bird). I forgot to mention that leading up to a final you may fight 2 or 3 times in a week to qualify and sometimes twice in one day. In May 1984 I was posted back to Germany to a place called Herford. Back at last in this lovely country and thrust straight into the boxing team only now at a higher level. We were entering the Corps (BAOR) competition along with the divisional competition against other Regiments/Corps.

Our RSM Jim Coffey had been a star of yesteryear and decided to rekindle the boxing throughout the Royal Corps of Signals which had been allowed to lapse for many years. Now this was fulltime training at its very best. Ex-Army champion trainer, food, conditioning, fitness, medicals etc. I fought in 1985 and 1986 in the Royal Signals BAOR finals and became the Middleweight champion on both occasions. I also reached the semi-finals in both years in the Divisional Championship. Losing both times to the Welsh (tough boys). Two things of note worth mentioning is that whilst progressing through the fights I fought a young man called Tony Velinor. He left the Army later to turn professional. Now boxing is a tough sport no matter what level you get to or take part in. Tony hit me so hard, it was the first and only time an opponent had such an effect on me. His power was awesome and I was no slouch either, needless to say he won the fight. The other fight worth mentioning was against an Army selected boxer, by that I mean he had represented the Army at boxing (I wanted to as well but was never selected). Well for two rounds I would have been better off fighting a shadow, don't think I managed to hit him once in those rounds. Such was his superior skill I could not touch him, yes he was also a bit cocky I thought. At the end of round two I returned to my corner where my trainer proudly announced that I had to knock him out to win (yes they really do tell you that!!). No shit Sherlock I thought, but as I have not laid a glove on him in the first two rounds what chance would I have of landing one in round three? I keep mentioning I am a very fit man and never took shortcuts in my training ever. Well mister pretty boy 'I am better than you' ran out of steam. I chased him, with no finesse, throughout round three and did manage to stop him. The look on his face was of total shock. I still have the fight on video.

So after the finals in May 1986 I decided it was time to change sport and see what else was on offer. They asked me later in the same year if I wanted to step up a level and fight at a higher grade. Anyone who has fought in a boxing ring no matter at what level will agree with the following points. The sport itself is physically demanding, the body is trained to a very high level, every muscle group is utilised in the training that leads up to each fight. Having fought over the last 6 years I had come to the conclusion (self-analysis) that I just did not have enough skill to do myself justice. Fit, strong and tough enough God YES. The question was, was I actually good enough? I officially retired from boxing at the tender age of 26, only returning as an A.B.A. (Amateur Boxing Association Coach) trainer in later years for other teams. So what could I do now?

Let me list some achievements I am proud of, I will elaborate on some of them later:

- Marathon 1986 **3hrs 33 Mins**, completed in the days when you had to wait and walk to the start line, I would guess that it took me at least 15-20 mins before I started running! Therefore actual running time would be approximately: **3hrs 15/18 Mins**

- Marathon on Roller Skis in Moenchengladbach Germany 1991 **2hrs 30 mins**, but I had to wait for 15 mins after the race had started so as not to get involved with the runners. It was an absolute blast, culminating in me receiving more newspaper coverage than the actual winner (a copy of which I have to this day)
- Half Marathon 1984 (Lage Bielefeld 88 mins
- 400 Metres.50.60 secs
- 800 Metres 2 Mins 4 secs
- 10 km 39 mins
- 2 miles relay race X4 people in each team: 11 mins 38 Secs
- Royal Signals BAOR Middleweight Boxing Champion 1985/6
- BAOR Divisional Semi Finals Boxing 1985/6
- BAOR Major Units Runners up Athletics 1988
- **GB National Bobsleigh Championships 1988/9 7th place UK**
- BAOR Major Unit Cross Country Champions 1991 1st Place team
- Army Junior Bobsleigh Championships 1991 3rd place
- GB National Bobsleigh Championships 1991 Crashed/injured/retired

I have taken part in 4 Marathons, 15+ half marathons, numerous 10k events and many athletics competitions along with a variety of Army challenges with and without packs on your back.

- **Three Peaks Challenge 2004 4th   placed team (21hrs)**

- Mount Snowdon (Top to Bottom PYG Track) 2007 1hr 55mins (I will beat it)
- Tough Guy 2007 3 hrs
- Clun Valley 25 miles 2007 7hrs 40 Mins
- Yorkshire 3 peaks 2007 11hrs (I will beat it)
- Everest Basecamp 2008 March/April 2008
- Grim Challenge (Aldershot) 2007/2011
- Mudrunner 2012

So what sport would appeal to me now boxing was over? Well in the Army it is an order to read 'Part One Orders' daily for information. In September 1986 they were asking for personnel to go to Fallingbostel in Germany to attend trials to be selected for the bobsleigh team. Well this sounded exciting and what the hell was bobsleighing?! The trials were held over a weekend and the top 20 personnel were selected to go back to England to Haringey sports club (big club in its day) for further evaluation and/or selection. Well fortunately I sailed through the trials and the next week went with the other 19 personnel to England for more tests.

I might add that at the beginning of June 1986 I had badly dislocated my right shoulder whilst playing in the Army 'Rugby Sevens' tournament in Herford (West Germany), my recovery however was swift, due mainly to my motivation. Anyway I again sailed through the trials and was selected to go to a place called Winterberg, in Germany, which is a refrigerated bobsleigh track to train on the ice to become a bobsledder. On the first day as part of a two man sled we were sat halfway down the track first as a driver then as a brakeman. They push you off and away you trundle at slow speed barely riding high in the corners. You are evaluated by the experts and on the second day go to the top of the track. They still sit you in and push you off from the top, now however everything is much faster and your reactions need to match. Some people took to it well and others crashed (you are told this is character building!). After one week of ups and downs some of us, me included, were selected to race in Igls, Austria in the novice championships. Point to note here is that a guy called Shaun Olsen (PARA) joined as a novice the same year. He became the British No1 for years and won a Bronze medal in the four man sled at the Nagano Winter Olympics in 1998.

Bobsleigh takes part in winter mainly, all races start around November time and end by February of the next year. Most tracks these days are refrigerated with the exception of Cervinia (Italy) and St Moritz. I raced on both tracks mentioned and it was an absolute thrill each time. It is a very costly sport both personally and from the sponsors. It was fortunate that the Army supported the sport along with Save & Prosper and Wincanton. As in all sports a lot of politics are involved, subsequently not all decisions made are always the best. That sentence is obviously open to conjecture, not to worry though still had a lot of fun. Me and my wife at the time became the first husband and wife team to race together in Austria in 1988/9. In the season of 1988/9 I finished 7th in the British National Championships and had high hopes for the future. Sadly in 1991 whilst taking part in the GB national qualifications I crashed in Koenigsee near Bertchesgarten and ended up with a badly dislocated left shoulder. That ended my bobsleigh career, an olive branch was offered in 1992 but I had decided to leave the Army so left it for someone else to have a go at a wonderful sport. It gave me lots of memories that I will cherish forever including practising with Prince Albert of Monaco in St Moritz and watching the great Sir Steve Redgrave trial in Winterberg. The tracks that I raced on were:

- Cervinia, Italy (natural track)
- St Moritz, Switzerland (natural track)
- Winterberg, Germany (refrigerated track)
- Igls, Austria (refrigerated track)
- Sarajevo, Yugoslavia (always cancelled due to communism!!)
- Thorpe Park London (dry training slope)

My qualifications gained as a serving soldier were as follows:
- Electrician Driver Class 1 (Plant Operator)
- HGV1 Licence
- Motorcycle Licence
- Forklift Reach & Counterbalance
- First Aid Instructor & Regimental Medical Assistant
- Small Arms Weapons Instructor
- Fieldcraft & Tactics Instructor
- Physical Training instructor
- ABA Boxing Coach
- Basic German
- Education for Promotion (5 Subjects)

Reunions so far attended, they originated from a group of soldiers meeting in a bar in Herford, West Germany called the **PIGS BAR** in the early to mid-1980s. The formula for remembering when they occur is simple, **the first weekend in June, 1200hrs at a location pre-decided**:

- 1995 Trafalgar Square 10 year reunion
- 2000 Blackpool Tower 15 year reunion
- 2005 Edinburgh castle 20 year reunion
- 2010 Cardiff Castle Gates 25 year reunion

And I hope to make the next one -

- 2015 Newcastle (St James Park) 30 year reunion

I left the British Army on October 1993, but continued to work for them as a civilian based in Germany.

**Boxing Championships 1985 Middleweight Final.
How to deliver a left jab to the head.**

**I won it again in 1986 against the same opponent, in
that same year I retired from boxing.**

Leadership course (Birgelen West Germany) 1986

100 metre sand hill called the fighting hill, the first one to the top did not have to go again. Trust me I did win (No. 18)!

**Winterburg (West Germany) 1988/89 (GB Squad)
(me = front left Bobsleigh)**

Very bad picture of myself having just taken part in the Great Britain Bobsleigh National Championships in Igls, Austria 1988/89 season finishing in a very creditable 7th Place in UK

January 1994 Aged 32 (Civilian)

Chapter V

<u>MUM & DAD</u>

Sadly as I was writing this chapter Mum passed away on 26th May 2006 and Dad passed away on 20th February 2007. I will explain more on that later as I believe the start should cover the story of two wonderful, fantastic parents. Many superlatives can be used to describe them both along with some that have not yet been invented. I do hope that this chapter does them both justice, as a married couple and as individuals.

Mum always used to say, "**<u>You will miss this voice when it's gone</u>**". My how does one start to explain the magnitude of that sentence? You would expect it to go without saying. I guess we will have to console ourselves with our own private thoughts whether good or bad. The only thing to say about the bad is that it should pale into insignificance when the good surely outweighs it. As a guideline, not that we need one, think of all the words of encouragement alone. Not forgetting being brought up in the circumstances that we were in with our Father. The love, the gifts, the monetary assistance, the reminders, life's guidelines and values, motivation, the list is bloody endless what this one woman selflessly gave to us all both collectively and more importantly as individuals.

Take a long look at the photos of them both and you can see firstly how beautiful our Mum was and from Dad's Army photo just how big and strong he was. Mum retained an air of elegance on each and every day that I was privileged to know her. She was meticulous in everything that she did, without a shadow of doubt a truly fantastic mother. In Chapter I, I told you that at an early age our father had an accident and became disabled. A condition that continued for almost 40 years, until he died.

So what do we say about them, first I will talk about Mum. As children Mum was very strict with us, something she told my oldest brother (Ace) and I that she regretted. We went to great pains to explain to her that in our opinion everything she did for us meant more than the times she told us off. Let's face it no one gave parents a book (unlike today) to explain how children were to be brought up. The values were instilled in our parents from their own parents. The things that they chose to change in the way they brought us up were their own choice. Yes Mum was strict at times but let's not forget the stress we as individuals placed upon her with our demands. Not forgetting that she also took the brave decision to look after Dad as well after his accident. So in effect when our youngest brother (Alexander) was born, after Dad's accident she had 5 of us to look after. From my personal memory I would say that Mum gave us all as many opportunities as she could, one give and two afford. We had no concept of the idea that we may have been missing out on anything at all, unlike in today's world where it seems to be accepted that to be a well adjusted person you must have it all. Things for Mum must have been very tight; it could not have been easy to bring up a family on disability allowance. Dad got no compensation for his accident (more on that in his part of the book). With all the knowledge that Mum had she gave to us and pushed us when we showed little interest. She would allow no one, and I mean no one, to call or comment on any of her family. God was she also house proud and until the day she died we were never allowed to walk into any room other than the kitchen with our shoes on. I feel sure that that comment will strike a chord with people everywhere. Mum was always cleaning, even when products became available to make life easier we could not stop her no matter how hard we tried. Mum was brilliant with money, she always had a little in reserve for that treat you had been begging for but thought you could never have.

Years ago when the January sales really were sales, Mum would start to buy presents for the next Christmas, continuing throughout the year. By the time Christmas got here we always had loads to open, she carried on with this tradition right up to her death. We always gathered at Mum's to dish out the presents and the Christmas of 2006 was extra special as, even though Mum had passed away, she had already bought and wrapped presents. My youngest brother lives in Mum's old house so it's a tradition we carry on as a family in her memory.

So what do we remember of this wonderful lady, let's put it into short phrases (not in any order) and allow you to fill in or create your own picture. Whilst doing so see if you can relate it to your own life either in a small way or maybe vastly similar. One thing is for sure parents all across our beloved world are doing their very best to raise families. I salute them all in what is a very tough arena; we know as we progress we don't always get it right. Not I believe due to a lack of effort on the parent's part (with exceptions to the rule):

- Music, something Mum enjoyed and indeed played almost every day. I believe that all the best records have already been made. Mum always had her mini stereo on in the kitchen. Do you remember the old stereos with the bale arm? We always put too many on and got told off. Mum introduced us all to music although our tastes did change as we grew older. One of my lasting memories of songs played to me by Mum was one called "Harper Valley PTA". I now have it on my phone and play it often when I'm thinking of her.

- From the music she even tried and I mean tried to teach us to dance, she had success with our sister. We boys however tried in vain.

- I don't think we give Mums or Dads enough credit for adapting to our very individual needs. Our constant demands along with our ever changing views must have been a nightmare for them both.

- Mum was always immaculately turned out each and every time she walked out of the door. We also were immaculate as she dressed us with pride whenever she took us anywhere. Especially if we were visiting relatives or friends.

- Meticulously clean throughout the house to the point of frustration sometimes. Remember when women used to clean their front door steps!! How many times must one hoover a house? Not knocking it I just don't understand why it was every day! Dusting as well, what about cleaning the windows with good old Windolene.

- Decision maker, many had to be made for us all as a family and individuals.

- Goodwill ambassador when we as brothers and sister flew off at each other and would not speak. Mum took her time to put things right, sadly at the end of her life she could not make our belligerent sister see the error of her ways. Always two sides to a story for sure, sadly she could not get through this time (more in our sister's very own chapter)

- The workload and effort required to bring up a family without all the mod cons we have in the world today. When they were available MUM stuck to her principal, once I can afford it we will have it and not until.
- What a figure for someone who had 4 children.
- Cooking, cleaning and nurturing our growth

I touched upon it in an earlier passage, but it's worth repeating again, how difficult do we make it for our parents with all the trials and tribulations that we put them through whilst growing up and often until the end of our or their lives. A long sentence I know but one that only required a full stop at the end of the statement no matter how long. Even if you are an only child we make it difficult for them at times, more than one child opens up a whole new arena of ideals, beliefs and transgressions for the parents to understand. Often comments in return are to guide us by people who hopefully have more experience. Not forgetting that they are not always right or accepted as such, but please don't forget that we as children are also often not right. It takes a strong person to turn round and say sorry we were wrong. Now at times our Mum had a torrid time, something that each one of us needs to take into consideration. Sadly we also pushed her hard; from my own point of view in my conversations with her I often said how proud I was to have her as my Mum. Mum never faltered in her determination to ensure that we were all happy and safe no matter what life threw at us. As anyone who may be reading this book knows, boy do we know, that life does not follow any script that has ever been written. Mum always pushed where necessary and offered pearls of wisdom as appropriate. She was often the dividing line between our fights with each other.

Looking after 4 children of varying ages in the 1960s plus a disabled husband must have taken all her strength. I believe Mum not only adapted to this struggle but achieved great success through it. Even with regard to our sister being divided, Mum fought until her dying day to put it right. Traits of Mum's character she gave to our sister were those of stubbornness and hatred. Hatred is probably too strong a word but when Mum disliked someone it would and could last forever. The reason I put that in is because Mum had an issue with Dad's family which she held until the day she died. We (brothers) have gone some way to make the peace with them because we did not agree with Mum's view point. But we did I must stress totally respect Mum's views, although as I said earlier, we may not have always agreed with them.

In today's world our Mum sacrificed everything and gave all her life to her family, my wish is that she was proud of what she achieved. I know from talking to Mum's friends that she often talked about us as a proud parent and of what we were doing or had achieved.

One hopes that the following point does not upset any member of my family in any way. Certainly no harm is intended at all. This is an observation based solely on my feelings about life and recollected thoughts. As I go through life I know how important it is to share it with someone who you love and adore (no matter what). At some times more than others you need to be held by the other person. Mum I think found that side of life lacking, I'm not sure if it was just Dad's way and I feel bad about making these comments in their absence without discussion. I got the feeling that Mum saw through us all as children then adults the way we interacted with our partners. It is my belief that Mum would have liked some TLC in her life. If Mum found it in any other way then I for one say fairplay to you. As mentioned before I think that throughout the years of Dad's disability they wore each other down to such an extent that at times it became unbearable. I also know that Dad would not blame Mum for anything because he told me so on my many visits to him in his care home. **One more thing that has to written is that Dad somehow blamed himself for Mum's sad death.** After she died he announced he no longer wanted to live and 9 months later he got his wish, hopefully joining Mum in the next life (bet they are arguing already!!)

Mum - as beautiful as ever

Mum with her friends in pose!

Mum and Dad

**Mum with her family, Alexander not yet born.
My was she a beautiful lady**

Mum in youthful pose

Mum and Dad (after his accident)

Mum aged 66, 3 days before she entered hospital where she fought valiantly for her life for 3 months until sadly she died.

Our beloved Mum fought valiantly for 3 months before she died, please allow me to explain exactly how it felt for myself only. If my brothers and sister felt any of the same then I will have explained it well. I feel sure that it will not be far off the truth for us all. Like each member of our close family I went to the hospital every day full of hope. My internal prayers each and every day were sounded out to whoever would or was listening.

Mum originally went into hospital with stomach pains, they diagnosed constipation at first. It turned out that her bowels had burst and she was being poisoned by her own body. Obviously they had to operate immediately. This filled Mum with horror as she hated to be unwell, that also included being in hospital.

We went home whilst Mum had her operation; obviously we would go back the next day and visit her whilst she made a magnificent recovery. Little did we know exactly how ill she was and indeed what internal damage had already occurred. At this point in time I would also like to say that Mum had been a smoker for upwards of 40 years. This sadly impeded her ability to recover.

Anyway we returned the next day to find Mum had been placed into the Intensive Care Unit. Of course we wanted to know why as it was a great shock to us all; apparently it was worse than anticipated. A doctor took us all to a room to explain the gravity of the situation. I myself sat listening from another world, cannot explain why I thought he was going to say something different to the fact that Mum would recover. To be fair he was quite sympathetic (natural in the circumstances). He further explained that some people do not recover from this operation. How bloody dare he say that? This was our mother; of course she was going to recover. Can I also point out that I am writing this just over 17 months after Mum's death. Well we came out of that room all with our own private thoughts but each in a total state of shock.

So each day we went into ICU and held her hand whilst talking to her, looking for any sign of response. Absolutely anything that was deemed a response became the next thing to focus upon. Incessantly we asked whichever nurse was on duty questions. They carry out tests on ICU patients periodically throughout the day, we clung onto absolutely anything positive.

We met other people we knew in the ICU unit who also were visiting relatives; one of them had had the same operation as Mum. Sadly however he did not wake up and very sadly after a number of weeks he died. Our thoughts and prayers are with his family and that of other families.

They decided to wean Mum off the sedative to see her response; she came round and opened her eyes. Tears of joy, would she be ok? I use the word would on reflection because I now know the answer to that question. Mum looked tired and was more than a little bewildered. We kept talking to her, being positive. But as quickly as they brought her round they had to sedate her again. Then she caught the dreaded MRSA bug and was placed in isolation. This occurred no less than three times in the 3 months she was in ICU. Well, just as I would guess is normal, we went for the jugular towards the hospital. Once again they had to explain the reasons behind MRSA and how it exists in all walks of life and within the hospital. Sadly we were not comforted by the explanation. But now Mum had something else to fight against. I mentioned smoking before; well Mum's lungs were filling up with residue which impeded her ability to fill her lungs with oxygen. They had to continually use a catheter to drain her lungs of fluid throughout each day. **Let that be a lesson to anyone**

who is considering smoking. To the people who smoke I would strongly advise them to consider stopping.

Once Mum was given the all clear from the MRSA they moved her back into the main ICU ward and again weaned her off the sedation. Mum was at all times receiving oxygen, something she relied upon and would not let go of. I'm not sure if Mum knew how serious it was (I suspect however she did) but she would not let them reduce the oxygen. I think Mum knew she would die if it was taken away, the body however cannot continuously keep receiving it. In order for the body to make a recovery it needs to do the work itself. Once this became a continual pattern it became difficult to believe Mum would survive. So now we had to go to the hospital, being positive knowing that the outcome of a full recovery was unlikely. But we do, I repeat we do have to have HOPE, for without it no one could recover from any illnesses or survive catastrophic situations (as our father survived his accident!).

As is true of almost all illnesses that result in death the patient at times seems to be making a recovery. This happened to Mum; I spent the whole of one visit animatedly explaining to her the detail of her illness from day one (this was about 6 to 8 weeks in). Mum was ever so bright that day; they had taken the tube out of her lungs and performed a tracheotomy. This helped her a lot in being able to allow her to try things for herself. Sadly however Mum was still dependant on the nurses. But I tell you her eyes that day were so full of life. Mum listened and nodded intently at my story of her illness; it was promised that upon a full recovery we would write to one of her favourite magazines and tell her story.

Tough decisions had to be made and we were informed that Mum would be moved to a ward, this effectively meant that they had run out of everything that they could do. After Mum was moved to a ward at George Eliot Hospital, the ward Sister met with us and told us that this was where she would stay until she died. Well the shock hit me hard, all along I think I knew but wanted so badly for it not to be the case. The visits were now getting harder, Mum had lost lots of weight and resembled someone who had spent time in a concentration camp. Sorry to use that as an analogy (I mean no offence to those that actually suffered this experience) but the despair was evident each day we visited. She would see us and lift up her frail arm for help. We knew she was going to die but still we had to constantly reassure her they were doing their very best. The level of care on a ward was pot luck, they were severely understaffed. Some of the nurses worked extremely hard but others were not so caring. They have all sorts of different coloured uniforms, this we found out meant that they could do some jobs but not others. Little wonder that the country feels undercut when receiving treatment. To be fair though they are now a results based organisation just like the rest of industry. Until we come away from this and make total care the priority then this will continue to happen. Anyway I digressed SORRY.

Mum died in the early hours on the 26 May 2006, we were called to the hospital but she died minutes before we got there. I gave Mum a kiss and said I look forward to meeting you again in heaven. **SO EMPTY NOW!**

Mum believed in life after death, we laughed over the years at this. Now however we are waiting for a sign, because if life after death does exist we will get one sooner or later. Things have happened such as

87

pictures being moved, hopefully this is a sign. I know in a dream early after Mum's death that we spoke, she told me that she had to let go because she was tired.

After Mum died as a family (3 brothers) we had to go through all her belongings and make the tough decision what to keep and what to move on. The things we found made us at times gasp in disbelief. The memories invoked came flooding back, how many pairs of shoes she had and most of them never worn. The clothes, many still brand new and covered in plastic. Why had we never noticed before, does anyone go into their parent's wardrobes to actually look, we never did. We shared some of the more treasured mementoes between us; the vast majority of things though went to the charity shop.

I would like to share with you all something of a revelatory find amongst Mum's papers, some form of poetry that Dad had written which Mum had translated for him. We also have some of the original copies that Dad himself wrote, which considering he was disabled is fairly legible. Whilst it will not make the Pulitzer prize, none of us knew that it existed, I am also not sure if it is one continuous poem or separate attempts:

Am I dead I woke up crying?
No she said but was she lying,
All around me there was space
But I couldn't put a name to any face.

Brain damage and lots of pain
And what's more he'll never walk again,
What a clout, I let out a shout
They don't know the man they are talking about.

All around me empty faces
But I know I'm going places,
The will to live is a mighty thing
And I will give it everything.

I would like to meet the girl again
Who joined me in my pain?

That sadly is where the first one ends. I think this relates to Dad's recollection of events after his accident when he was surrounded by people trying to save his life

What is this thing inside of me?
Forever yearning to be free,
Fears have tried it
Tears have plied it
The glory that is in me

Heaven sent it must have been
But should I believe it sight unseen,
Powers to be will question me
But might is the reason
And that is me

That is where the second one ends - The next ones are in Dad's own handwriting

As I watched them standing there
Sitting crippled in my chair,
Have I two heads, or an ugly face
What am I doing in this place?

They don't mean to be unkind
But just what do they have in mind,
Empty faces look upon me, meaningless words
speak to me
But can't they see I want to be free.

My life is to be spent in a chair
But that's no reason to despair,
Why can't they smile at the world?
If all life unfurled

Sadly again that's where it ends, not even sure if it's all supposed to be one!

Underneath the branches of a massive tree
It can't move, yet who is free,
The wind can move it
But can't shift me,
Who will know me when I've gone?
In this world I dwelt upon,
Who will know my fears and tears?
As I live on through my allotted years,
We don't ask to be born
So why in our innocence does god put us with liars
and false people?

I think if we had seen these before we may have encouraged him to have another look, then again it's exactly what he wrote and we have no power to change or alter any of it. Not that we would anyway, Dad's thoughts, Dad's work.

OUR FATHER

On February 10th 1937 our beloved father was born, we met him ourselves as we too came into this world. In this short passage how do we sum it all up, the LOVE – the PRIDE – the AFFECTION – we all felt in having him as our father. From childhood to now our love for him remains strong.

A message here to all with fathers (and mothers), never let it be too late in your lives to tell or show your parents just how much you love and appreciate them. We told ours regularly because without their undying love and support we would not be the people that we are today. We are all appreciative of just how complicated things seem sometimes.

For those who know our family and have shared our history throughout you will know that our lives as a family changed forever in 1968 when Dad had a life threatening accident. He was actually killed in the accident but such was his strength to live he fought through and survived to the point where he told the Vicar at the scene to go away and stop giving him the last rites. A story Dad often shared with us when we asked him about the accident. Our Mum took a faultless decision to have Dad back home where we settled down into life with a disabled father in a world that little understood what it was like.

Our life as a family was constantly adapting to Dad's needs, especially in recent years when his disability regressed, just as we were told it would nearly 40 years ago. We sincerely trust that our Dad was afforded the same depth of fatherhood from us all as any able bodied father receives. The only advantage we remember which we shared with Dad later in his life was that if punishment was given out at home we would rather Dad do it than Mum because of his disability he could not smack us as hard as Mum could.

We can never be 100% sure of just how it must have felt for our Dad to be disabled from his point of view especially if you see (from photos) just how big and powerful he was as a young adult. The absolute 100% point we can be sure about is that we each loved him and from that total respect emanates. His words of wisdom as we individually sought them helped us understand issues we could not ourselves get through with our thought processes alone.

Dad shared many words of wisdom with us as we grew up, some we little understood until later in our lives as we developed as people. I would like to share just a few with you, if you listen carefully to them and, as Dad would say keep it simple, we believe they will help you through life:

- Never let an excuse be the reason why you don't do it
- Live every day as though it's your last
- You can do anything you want to do, if you want to do it
- It's all in the mind, it can say yes and it can say no (equally)
- Keep it **SIMPLE**
- Man will eventually destroy this WORLD that we live in

Dad's absolute favourite aimed at people who always seem to have a bad day (and this from a man who was disabled) was:

- **EVERY DAY IS A GOOD DAY IF YOU WAKE UP ALIVE**

FUNERAL SPEECH

Dad would not want anyone to be sad today, he would want us and you all to pick ourselves up and move on into what can and should be a fulfilling life. We ask that you remember your conversations with him.

Dad did not have any bad words to say about anyone. Where he did not understand he offered a reason for it which in itself was a great lesson which we could always use. Tolerance and understanding was always what he taught us.

We feel sure that like us you will each have your own memories of our Dad, as well as today transfer them to your own lives from time to time and put right anything that is wrong no matter how long it takes. Now a short poem that for us sums our life up with Dad.

OUR HERO

We shared your life, thanks from us for that
A life we would not change no matter what,
A tower of strength you proved to be
We threw it all at you; we got through it as WE,
Our lives were full, as rich as any other
Your faultless application, it was never any bother,
The love, the laughs all that we shared
Was more than we could ever have dared,
Our love for you it never faltered
The life you gave to us we would never have
altered,
Now that you're with Mum, please say hello
We miss her too; we will see you both when it's our
time to go,
Our memories remain and we will tell all who will
listen
Of the father who made our lives absolutely glisten,
The words of wisdom that you gave to us all
Will assist in our journey as we walk tall,
As this ode ends Dad remember for us as a family
You were to us our very own **HERO**

These last two pages were what we three brothers wrote at the request of the vicar, and which my brothers kindly agreed I could say at his funeral. In a nutshell it seemed to capture our thoughts about a man whom we dearly loved for a whole variety of reasons. It would be too easy to let it lie at the fact that we spent a lot of our lives looking after him and adapting to his constant needs. His drive and lust for life need also to be told. So let's begin to talk about a man who we mostly knew as disabled.

As stated earlier Dad became disabled when myself, my elder brother and newly born sister were very young. Just because he was disabled he was still a father in every sense, although I suspect that in a small way we took advantage of the fact sometimes in our home life. That's not to say that we could take advantage because Mum would not let us do that anyway (a tough cookie on discipline). Dad dealt with his disability admirably although towards the end of his life we think he had had enough of it. Especially when he could not even stand up, that alone seemed to dampen his spirits as well as Mum losing her fight for life (for which he blamed himself).

Well from the Army photo you will see that as a young man Dad was very big and strong. It was due to this strength that he survived an accident which killed him at first; they brought him back to life. His will to live was demonstrated when he told the presiding vicar to stop giving him the last rites as he intended to live (only not as polite). Dad was on strong tablets when he first came home, to control the shakes and possible fits. He believed strongly until the day he died that if you want to do something you can, it's all in the mind. To that end all you had to do is tell your mind what to do (and not the other way round) and simply do it. This he applied throughout his life to absolute 100% perfection.

It included weaning himself off the tablets, stopping smoking, walking again (until the time he physically could not), stopping drinking, etc. Mind over matter also plays its part in my own life to this very day. Keep it simple he always said. People tend to over complicate things, hence why lots of people fail. You can do anything you want to do if you want to do it; to Dad it was that simple. Why others could not apply it was a continual bewilderment to him. Please don't forget that although Dad was disabled, the thought process never waned throughout his life. I cannot lie and say that we wished things were not different for him. We can say however that we are totally grateful that he survived and that Mum brought him back home. The rest we made up as a family as we moved along in life.

As we grew we became the arms and legs for Dad as he asked us to do things with him, the things he could not, such as:

- Gardening, growing more food than a farmer and each year as our friends passed our garden we used to give them bags of vegetables. A tradition I wished still existed today and would make neighbourly coexistence a whole lot better. Perhaps we would even talk to each other!
- Writing things for him, letters, betting slips, etc
- Building rockeries under his guidance ;
- Collecting his newspapers.
- Feeding him later in life
- Walking with him (well that meant me in the early years)
- Operating technology; he was dumbfounded by it until the day he died. He never got the hang of Sky TV and its many channels
- Toilet duties (Mum and myself only)

Life in my opinion was great; Dad was always looking to push himself after his accident. I guess later in life that's what frustrated him when he no longer could. We completed a 20 mile walking challenge a few years after his accident which he was proud to have finished. He would walk anywhere and everywhere, especially if you told him he could not, sadly this did not always have the best outcome, as mentioned earlier, he broke his nose no less than 10 times after falling over.

So we grew up and my older brother and I joined the Army and left home and country for the next 21 and 13 years respectively. Mum and Dad got posh and had a phone installed at home so we made weekly calls and visited throughout all those years. They were both an inspiration, giving us all continual guidance and total support. Well over the years as Dad's disability regressed we adapted accordingly. Utilising the following:

- Stairlift ;
- Electric Wheelchair ;
- Various walking apparatus.
- Manual wheelchair

Mum called us one time and said you will need to talk to your Dad and explain to him why we have to stop him using his electric wheelchair. Dad used to go out in it on his own and we were oblivious to the problems until helpful comments were reported back to Mum. Dad was crossing the roads but due to his disability, remember his brain had difficulty in telling him to stop at a zebra crossing or road edge, so he kept going. Don't get me wrong his brain could send a signal but by the time it got to his hands he was already in the road. Some kind car owners who knew him told my Mum, now we had the difficult task of telling Dad we were going to have to limit his independence. A decision I can assure you he did not take very well. He got around it initially because my daughter was so young she used to sit on his lap and steer for him. They were the talk of the town for a while especially when people saw how my daughter helped going in and out of the shops. But when it did sadly come to an end and we sold the wheelchair Dad did not talk to us for a while, he gradually came round.

Just before I returned to England we decided to bring Mum and Dad out to Germany for one last holiday with us all. During a phone call Mum said "Dean I do not want you to be upset but Dad's disability has really regressed". When they arrived it became clear what Mum meant, Dad went to the toilet using a walking frame. A distance of less than 25 feet that took him almost 10 minutes to cover. So shocked was I that I cried in front of all the people gathered. Sadly he was now regressing at an alarming rate.

I came back to England and settled in London, found a job on shifts and one day out of every shift I was off, I would drive home for the day and take Mum and Dad out for a meal. One could see that Mum was becoming tired and drained from the constant demands of looking after Dad with no help from anyone but family. I decided that I would take Dad away on holiday to give Mum a break. This I did and took him most years to his favourite place in the Lake District (Wrynose Pass). We stayed at Centre Parcs in Windermere, touring and exploring other places as well. Dad was comfortable with me, especially when carrying out his toilet duties. I too was comfortable in carrying this task out for him with dignity. My brothers although they assisted left it to me although I feel sure they could have done it as well.

Another thing I told Dad about was Sky TV, not having it he announced, bloody rubbish, too expensive.

When you consider that most of Dad's days were now spent watching TV I thought he would have jumped at the chance. Undeterred I booked an engineer and had it fitted. Thereafter he was like a child with a new toy; he could watch his beloved Spurs play football and any other sport he now wanted. I paid for him to receive Sky TV for 15 years, until his death and I dearly wished I could pay for another 15 years just to have him here. Technology was a constant bewilderment to Dad; we were always reminding him that he had more channels than he thought he had.

Dad was an avid reader throughout his life and a learned man with it; he often dropped pearls of wisdom into our lives. Often you would be sitting with him and all of a sudden he would give his point of view randomly. Sometimes on things you had discussed days or weeks earlier. Like Mum he would not have a bad word said about anyone of us. Even telling us all off when we commented on our sister after the arguments. Sadly questions he needed to raise with our sister, his daughter will forever remain unanswered as she did not visit him in the last year of his life. These questions that will remain are the reason why I (Dean) personally will have nothing to do with her ever again. Dad did not deserve to die without getting answers from her; she was too brazen to give him the time of day even when he spent 10 days fighting for his life. She knew he was in hospital but made no attempt to visit him, no doubt she will blame us boys but we would never have stopped her seeing him.

Dad spent 10 days in ICU fighting for his life having been resuscitated initially in A&E. Dad had to endure a tracheotomy on the 2nd day, far different to the first one nearly 40 years before when it was quite revolutionary. They had to sedate Dad a lot because he kept trying to pull the tube out. I spoke to him before they sedated him on day 4 after which he never woke again. I was visiting on my own and he looked at me, I asked him "did he know that we all loved him", he nodded yes and as God is my witness dropped a tear from his left eye. I feel sure that Dad knew he was not going to make it, just to be stubborn though he survived at a very high temperature for a few days before he died. It was his last fight with life and a very big loss to this day. We miss him and Mum terribly but are comforted by the fact that we were able to share each other's lives until the day they both left us. One day we will all be reunited and hopefully they can sort this family mess/turmoil out. Dad died in the early hours of 20 February 2007, we arrived to hold his hand before he left us.

I still talk to both of my parents to this day and will continue to do so until I die. Also I have broken down and cried more than once often spontaneously. Once whilst shopping with my wife I burst out crying. One assumes it is grief, Mum's photo is by my bed and I say good night every night. Dad's photo is in my office, he is watching me now typing this book on my PC. I wait and look for signs that they are still in my life, they are here somewhere and they will be forever in my heart. And to think when I was younger I used to laugh at Mum saying these things, hope she is listening or reading this.

Sadly the care home that Dad resided in did not even bother to send a condolence card, three of the carers did come to Dad's funeral but as for the rest!!

Since both Mum and Dad died it has left an empty void, questions I used to share and discuss with them both are now discussed in my mind. I would dearly love to speak to them both again as I used to. Topics for discussion were varied, simple and complex in content. On ad-hoc occasions I am overwhelmed by a deep sadness that the questions that constantly spring to mind cannot be discussed with them. Some of my friends lost their parents early in life, my sympathy was extended but I never truly knew how they felt about it. Now I think I have an understanding, absolutely empty of the two people who gave me life, love, guidance and understanding at all times. Each time I read this chapter it makes me feel sad inside, it also serves as a reminder that life for us all is constantly moving. I truly want to make you understand that I feel these are the best parents ever written about. But hopefully you are also thinking the same about yours. Remember what I put at the beginning? The good should outweigh the bad, if it does then believe me you're onto a winning formula. All our efforts should be put into making the world a great place for everyone, young and old.

Dad as a baby

Dad aged 18 as a recovery mechanic in the R.E.M.E. during National Service

Dad on exercise in West Germany

Dad working on the railway

Dad at home in the kitchen on return from hospital, after his accident. If you look closely at the photo you will note the indentation in his throat caused by a tracheotomy

Dad at one of his favourite places, the farms at the back of Bermuda Village, you would not know that he was disabled until you saw him walk!

Mum and Dad in London

Dad with his boys

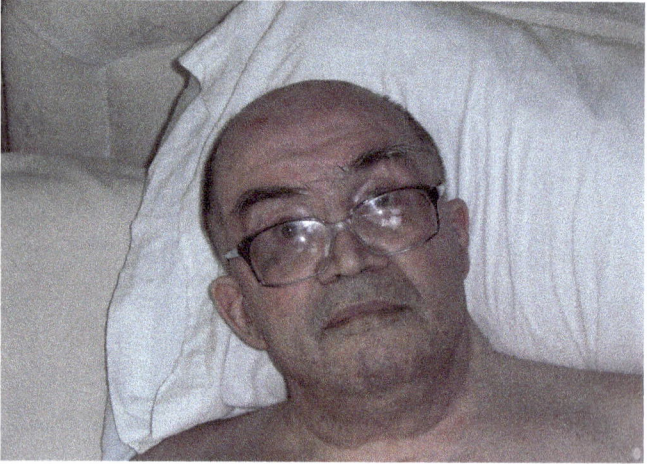

Dad in the care home (notice the tell-tale chocolate marks around his mouth from his favourite Ritter Sport Halbbitte flavoured chocolate) almost 70 years old

I shared many thoughts throughout the years of talking with Dad; he also shared many things with me. As the years passed the things we talked about became more and more personal and I didn't expect some of the thoughts that we shared. I often told Dad that I loved him and I truly meant it. One thing I do wish to make comment about is my Dad's childhood.

- First of all Dad was always a bit of a rebel, no stronger comment than that do I make. That will be for others to remember who may read this
- As a war child he was always getting into trouble, one occasion was taking things form a wreckage of a downed aeroplane

I have separated this next point; before I share with you what he told me let me also add some background to it. My Dad according to himself, friends and family members did not get along well with the word authority or those that displayed it. Although I take nothing away from what he told me, equally I feel sure that at times his part in the process is not beyond question.

Dad told me that he dreaded his own father coming home. His father would work hard all day then go to the pub for a drink or two. Upon returning home he would ask Eric (my Dad) to come into the room where he then proceeded to beat him. Please note that I only have my father's side of the story and feel sure that he may have done something to deserve this treatment. Not that this excuses what happened, there isn't anything in today's world that would be treated less abhorrently. These beatings occurred quite regularly. If you look at my Dad's photos he was a big man, at the age of 15 he looked like the photo of him when he was 18. One day when his father came home and asked for him, before he could start hitting him, my Dad hit him first. Apparently my Grandfather fell and was unconscious for a short while. I know my father regretted it to the end of his days, equally I know that he loved his father as any man should. He did not pre-judge him whatsoever, but he did not like being hit almost daily. He was never beaten again.

Although this should take up more writing space I will keep it short and simply add that we are building bridges every day. Our relationship with Dad's family was somewhat strained due to our Mother. She did not stop us visiting them but she herself very rarely came with us. At weekends we used to visit Grandma and Granddad Horobin, the great joy here for me was Grandma's cake box which was the single most reason why I visited. Grandma was always inquisitive and keen to hear our news. Granddad never said much really, mainly he just sat in his chair almost as head of the house. I sincerely wished I had more to say but sadly I do not, suffice to say that they are very kindly thought of. I will never forget the upset in Auntie Margaret's eyes when Grandma died. As stated later "life is best understood backwards, but must be lived forwards".

"LIVE EVERY DAY AS THOUGH IT'S YOUR LAST"

When Mum & Dad died a part of me went with them, never to be forgotten XXX

Chapter VI

Brothers and Sister (Evil) Mum's Only Daughter

I have decided to spend the first part of this chapter on our sister and to tell where we are at in our lives today. Her name is Samantha and she was the third born child. After having two boys Mum was anxious to have a daughter. One assumes it was to allow her to have a child with affinity to her own sexual orientation as a female. Mum certainly wanted a girl to spoil throughout life but she was in for a bad return from her, especially later in life when the bigger picture became clearer. Still as a child it was much easier for Mum to control things (or so she thought). It has to be said that we think Mum did gain a lot from having a daughter, but their relationship was severely tested over the years. I need to make it quite clear that this is our side of the story along with many conversations with some of Mum's very dear friends. Our sister will obviously have her own version of events.

Well as a child I guess Mum had her little girl who she could make a fuss of, we were never left out I may add. She was a very demanding child and teenager, constantly wanting things. Not a lot different from other kids I hear you say, the answer to that is both YES and NO. It's how you make demands, sulking, threatening, etc. and later in life telling blatant lies for self-gain. Now those are harsh words, it is hoped that I write this well enough to give reasoning for such strong statements.

Samantha was a very highly driven child, this developed in her teenage years and most certainly as an adult in business. There is nothing wrong with being driven unless of course it hurts or affects the people that you love and care about. The demands for Mum to get her anything and everything resulted in a lot of sulking and pressure applied, especially as a teenager. The use of threats was common place; these got worse as she got older when she seemed to care less and less who she was upsetting. Mum would have given her the world and how she did try, constantly driven by the demands of a very selfish (unhappy) young lady. Mum fed her every request even when it meant going more than the extra mile. I say unhappy because Samantha confided in me many times that she was unhappy both in her work and private life. One point to add is that I and my elder brother Ace had both left home to serve in the Army by the time Samantha became a teenager.

Samantha met Ben who became her husband and father to two wonderful children and all was happy for a while. That was until he took it upon himself to swear at our mother. It was Mum that stopped me and my older brother from returning home from Germany to knock ten bells of SH*T out of him. My older brother wrote a letter asking him to apologise. Our sister's response to all this was to announce she wanted nothing more to do with our family and off she went. This caused a great deal of upset to our Mum but we, her three sons, rallied round to keep her spirits up. We didn't see or hear from Samantha again for almost four years. Meanwhile she had had a son (Maxim) whom we first met when she returned to the family. So all settled down and we got to know each other again. Our sister had now become a snob, for want of a better way of putting it, appearing embarrassed about her upbringing and her family. I state that this is my opinion only.

Our Mum was very good with money, she always seemed to have some saved for a rainy day, and our sister took advantage of this over the years. Mum gave her thousands of pounds, a fact I feel sure that our sister will deny. That being the case then I will gladly ask her to answer the questions behind the many receipts that I have clearly showing that Mum gave money to her and the reasons why? The deposits for houses that our sister owns. Now you might think that I am bitter and I have to admit I am a little but not about the money just the lack of honesty about it. However all that I write has come from the mouths of highly respected family members and friends. One person who visited Mum every week (above 20 years) right up to the day she died and without prompting told me all about the money at our Mum's funeral. Our sister even tried to upstage Mum's day at the funeral, which all family members commented was sad.

Our sister had her own companies which she was constantly growing and then stripping of assets and, more importantly, upsetting a lot of people along the way. This never mattered as the only person Samantha cared about was herself. She bought a lot of property for investment, including shops for business. Nothing I might add was ever given to our parents (not that she had to you understand). She will tell you that she offered but seeing is believing in my book. I even went into the property business with her, we bought a house together but a year later she forced me to sell her share. So her input was £8,000 and a year later she received £17,000 in return. An investment many people would like to be involved in. Selling the property was not really the issue but the lies she told certainly were. Lies she could not stop especially in later years as they got bigger and she nearly cost me my job.

When Mum became ill our sister suddenly became the loyal daughter. Mum's operation was very serious. In fact 3 months later she sadly lost her fight for life and died. Anyway, as soon as Mum was admitted to hospital Samantha announced that she would look after her finances and pay the bills whilst she was in. That was ok we had no reason to suspect anything, except as we later found out that Mum had a document case highlighting every monetary event. This case spent the first few weeks at our sister's house and only came back when our eldest brother found out that they were not paying any of the bills. So she sent her husband to give the case back to us under a very big cloud. On inspection we found that documents had been re-arranged or were missing, what we have pieced together gives the reason behind an earlier question. Let her answer the questions behind the money against the remaining documentation that we have. This also includes the deposits for her houses that we all know Mum gave to her.

Our Mum left no will because she was scared to, thinking that she would die if she made one. One of our cousins asked her to make one a week before she was admitted to hospital, as a precaution to the events we found ourselves in. The people I do feel sad for are her children and my brother's children who are missing being part of a bigger family. What exactly did our Mum do wrong? In today's world of constantly asking questions what the bloody hell did our Mum do to her other than love and help her? Unfortunately only my sister knows the answer. I suspect we will never know, anyway she did something far worse which means I personally will never spend time with her again. Will we ever forgive her? The answer is probably yes, but what we cannot do is ever forget, which makes it impossible at this moment in time for any reconciliation. I feel sorry for her children as I really enjoyed being part of their lives.

So what did she do to our father? Well she questioned how our mother could sleep with a disabled man. What I might ask has that got to do with her? It is an opinion that she had, she also had no respect for our father as she regarded him as unintelligent. She rarely visited him for long and never offered to ever take him on holiday (she had a bad back and a weak husband). My story though only covers the last two years of his life, which he spent in a care home because Mum could no longer cope with Dad at home. In the last year of his life, including the 10 days he was in hospital and his funeral she never visited him and could only be bothered to send a wreath. She interred Mum's ashes without my Dad or any of her brothers being there. Something Dad never understood up to the day he died. She took and kept Mum's rings which belonged to Dad and dispatched the obligatory solicitor's letter to tell him they were hers and she would not be giving them back. Not forgetting the 'do not contact me or my family again'.

Now on to what she did to me and my brothers, it was decided that as Dad could not look after his own affairs I would obtain Powers of Attorney and do it for him. She accused me of stealing, contacting the fraud squad who instantly froze my bank accounts and visited my home to question me. This was all sorted out within 4 hours of me producing all the evidence that I had showing that I had carefully followed every process explained to me in law.

I almost gave up my job to work for Samantha but at the eleventh hour she announced the directors did not want a family member working for them. I later found out that she employed her husband because he had lost his own job, not a problem, but no explanation just more lies. She also told the police that I threatened her daughter at the hospital during visiting. All witnesses will show that it was my sister who threatened me and my wife. The Christmas before all this happened I took her daughter and son to London for a few days showing them the sites and taking them to the theatre. We stayed in a hotel with no problems whatsoever. She also slated both my brothers, the oldest being Neanderthal and the youngest being a liar. Not forgetting how perfect she was herself!

Now you learn a lot as you go through life as an individual and a family member, it was not my wish to ever comment on my family other than that said in an earlier chapter. That is that we are all different but somehow we have to make it work. I know both Mum and Dad would be upset that we are at war, a war which was started before both their untimely deaths. And yes many times we tried to resolve it but she (our sister) would have none of it. It is our belief that she truly thinks that she is better than us all. All we are guilty of is making our way through life as best we can. She has also upset numerous employees and directors in her wake with the incessant lies and stories. One firm summoned her to a meeting and whilst she was with them they changed the locks to her business which she had part sold to them. Now what does that tell you?

This happens to most families I hear you say, the answer is yes it does. So it's now open to interpretation. All we ever wanted was to have a peaceful life and share what we have with each other throughout it. Sadly sheer greed has forced our sister in a different direction. Our younger brother bought Mum and Dad's house for them and currently resides there. My older brother and I allowed him to use some of the money Mum left to make substantial changes to it. Today it's beautiful, we could all have had an equal share of the money but myself and Ace decided it would be better spent in respect of our parents. Today if Mum and Dad are watching they will enjoy my brother's two young girls growing up and having as much fun as we did.

My two brothers, Ace the eldest is exactly that and sees himself as a guide to us all, like a patriarch in the animal (elephant) world. Mum would be pleased; he was a Mummy's boy (sorry mate). Alexander, or the baby as we often refer to him, was equally close to Mum and Dad. As brothers we have had our fair share of ups and downs, at times major arguments. That said as we get older we have reached a calm, level of understanding, we still look out for each other and will if we feel necessary make a comment. Not always the correct one, as stated earlier I spent a lot of time with my elder brother during my time in the Army. Alexander was 11 when I left the country, we grew with him as he grew older, most definitely the calmest one of us all. In fact he is so laid back you would think he was dead at times. We often joke that we met him late in life when upon sitting down on the settee at home this lump moved and was introduced as our youngest brother.

Now as brothers we all have our strengths and difference of opinion, even today when one of us does something that the other dislikes we tell each other. Sometimes vehemently but never to the point of actual violence. For me it's the little things and changes I see in them which make me smile. Things that I never noticed earlier in life but seek comfort in now. Ace surprised me recently in his comments about Mum and Dad. It is difficult to know what is going on with my older brother, for whatever reason he rarely tells you. Sometimes however his guard does drop and he reveals a different side to him. I was visiting him and in his front room he has a picture of Mum and Dad. He shared with me that he misses talking to them but that he still speaks to them in his thoughts each day and, like me, would love to see them again. Now I never thought that he would not miss them, but he has never been very open with his feelings. I have no such hang ups, and am more of an open book. We had a lovely conversation about them, which I sought to share with my wife when I returned home.

The support we have given each other over the years has I hope been welcome and effective.

ACE (Arthur Charles Eric) Horobin

My oldest brother Ace is too often a closed book, whether he undersells himself or not is hard to tell. You almost never know what it is he is truly feeling, then all of a sudden like a bolt out of the blue he will converse with you eloquently and sensibly, minus the jokes. As he gets older this seems to be occurring more.

Thought I would get the opening off my chest first, can't say that we were that close as we grew up. Although he is just 17 months older than me as we were growing up it might well have been 17 years. More so when he left school and started to make his way in the world and I was still a teenager at school. He was definitely a Mummy's boy though, always telling tales, the family super grass. If Mum ever wanted to know where Dean was or should not be, just ask Ace!

It is my belief that he revelled in being the older brother and at 6ft 3 one of the tallest at school. Although we are quite close in age the gap did seem bigger when he left school and could go to places that I could not. Don't know why I was in such a rush to grow up, I wish it would go more slowly now I am in my 50s.

Our lives became closer as brothers after he joined the Army and I followed a year later. Indeed we spent our first tour together with him looking after me, especially after my first marriage broke up. Indeed Ace started his working career as pit worker, in those days the money was very good. He had his own posh car (Sunbeam Rapier, twin carbs!) and each night he came home from the pit it looked like he had put eye liner on his eyes. Boy did we take the P*ss. Then Ace and his good friend Michael Hood decided to join the Army, only trouble is that during separate interviews Ace joined the Royal Corps of Signals and Mick joined the

Royal Corps of Transport. Do you think they actually spoke to each other and decided which part of the Army they were going to join? To be fair they were probably coerced by the interviewing soldier.

I think that after my divorce he took it upon himself to look after me until I developed my own career. By that I don't mean he became a mother but I was very much included in his life in Germany. We spent many a weekend touring and drinking all over Germany. We had lots of fun with Army colleagues and all the bierfests (beer festivals) we attended. Not to mention a few fights with the natives along the way; we got into some real scrapes for sure. Even when he met his wife I was included and ended up going out with her friend Susanna for a while.

Like an elephant Ace sees himself as the family patriarch, always on the look out for any issues to resolve. He does not however do this in a tactful manner, often choosing the wrong words. Unless you know how to work with him you would think he was being awkward. Just goes to show that first impressions do not always count, a little perseverance might be better suited to the occasion.

He is however set in his ways, to some degree I think that we all as humans are. Ace though will not deviate from his routines, for love nor money. Ace can also be an angry man at times, for reasons he could change in my opinion. If only he could see that there is more to life than just being a provider. For sure he works hard for long hours, but even with that he is angry.

His eldest daughter Jasmine is now a mother herself, making him a grandfather to a little boy named Kevin. Ever since his marriage came to an end he has always sent money to his girls. This obligation normally stops in the UK at 16, but as his girls are German (his ex wife

122

Petra was German) he had to pay until they were 18. He still sends money direct to them, Jasmine is now 25 and Carmen 21. His love and effort cannot be faulted or questioned. That said I do wish he would take his foot off the gas a little and visit them more. He will miss out unless he changes his attitude and realises that life is not just about himself and his woes. I have no contact with my daughter and am very envious of his position. In my opinion he should visit them a whole lot more than he does, and stop using work as a bloody excuse versus cost to make the effort. We are all going to be dead for a very long time, seize the opportunities whilst still able to do so.

Looking as an outsider I cannot make my mind up if he is truly happy or not, you're right in thinking it has little to do with me. However I do care and would like to be able to talk to him about it, the only obstacle being Ace himself. The minute you suggest something he rears up like a lion for no reason, in my opinion (bloody word).

Whatever it is that he is holding on to he needs to release it and live his life rather than just existing. Who knows he may read this and make the effort, he may also tell me where to go. It's my book remember, whilst I don't wish to hurt anyone I feel it right to add this.

His inability to move on with life and relax more to my mind makes him so like our Mum. She was exactly the same; neither of them having any scope for negotiation. Once their respective minds were made up that was it, whomever it was aimed at it stayed aimed. If only he would take a look at himself and realise the consequences of some of his actions. Of course I never had any of these thoughts about him and his life until I applied the same logic to mine. Even now I cannot make him understand, perhaps if I write it down he might read it and understand.

Well over 7 years ago I became fed up with drinking alcohol as I suspected that I had a problem. I discussed this issue with our Dad, true to his usual form he helped guide me but not by telling me what to do. Instead he made me realise that if I truly wanted to stop drinking then I could. As stated earlier Dad gave me a strong mind and more importantly showed me how to work on it and make it understand that I had the power over it, if I chose to. With this in mind it quickly became apparent that I could not tell the difference between 1 and 20 drinks. In turn this meant my only choice was to stop altogether (Chapter X). I too have a temper, I too quickly fly off the mark, however I am trying hard to work on this on a daily basis. Even I get it wrong; 'who doesn't?' I hear you ask. Ace even questions why I need to go to AA meetings and support not only myself but others. The reason is, is that I will not know until the day I die if I have been successful with my quest to never drink again. After all I am only 7 years into my journey but so far it is great.

My point with the above paragraph is to highlight to my brother that we all have issues but some of us choose to try and overcome them. Again some will not be successful, but you cannot pour scorn on anyone who at least tries to alter feelings/anger/etc. Mainly by recognising the issues and more importantly by doing something about it.

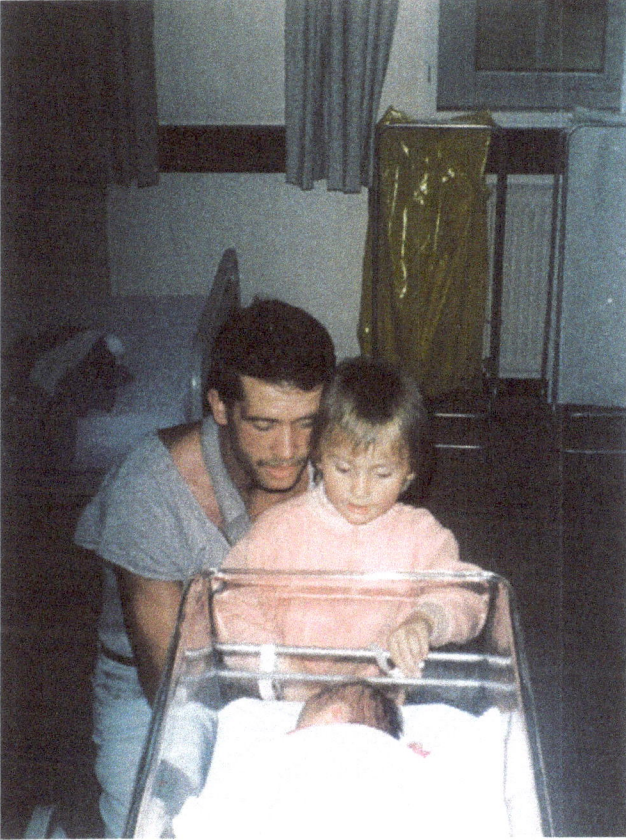

At the hospital with my brother Ace's eldest daughter Jasmine (now 25 and a Mother herself) peering into the cot at her newly arrived sister Carmen (now 21) in West Germany. Note the sling on my shoulder, recovering from yet another injury

Alexander Scott Horobin

If I was to comment on him at his age today (41), I would say that he is a bit of a dreamer. He is always a very smart young man, a little lazy but always dreaming of how to become the next millionaire. He has however a remarkable charm about him and has the ability to charm the pants off you. Perhaps this is why over the years he has gained some success from being a salesman and with women. He could truly sell you nothing and it would convince you it will be the next best thing that you own. Hopefully, not to the point of being a conman though.

Alexander is not able to do more than one thing at a time; he does not cope well with overloading. Today it is called multi-tasking, but not for Alexander.

Ace and I both left home to work whilst Alexander was still a very young boy, with 11years difference between our ages (add 17months on for Ace). I sadly don't know too much about his early years at home because we were not there. We brought him all the latest presents from Germany which were different to ones you would find in England. I know from talking to Mum he was a little envious of us being away working and in the jobs that we were doing. Indeed when Alexander became of age he considered joining the Army but we both talked him out of it. Purely because we did not think it would suit him, plus the Army was changing, as it should I may add.

He was and is always proud of his appearance, throughout his formative years he was always very smart. He certainly owned more suits than I will ever see or own. Always very well presented which I assume is looked upon highly by ladies. He certainly seemed to be popular with them when he came of age.

He is along with his partner Cat a parent to two girls **Caitlin and Emerson**, as different as chalk is to cheese. He needs to realise that his daughters are fast growing up and if he does not get involved (more) he will miss it all. It may just comeback to haunt him, one hopes not though. I could be wrong equally, cover all angles (coward)

I have no doubt that he loves his girls, a little less partying in front of them would not go amiss. Take them away at weekends instead of inviting his so called friends around for beer and the sort of antics most children do not need to see or experience. Again like my eldest brother he may read this and take some action. Not forgetting that he might actually disagree with my comments.

Countries and Places I have had the pleasure to visit:

- Barbados – Bridgetown – around the island
- Jamaica – Montego Bay – around the island
- Dominican Republic
- Mexico – Cancun
- Balearic Islands – Magaluf – Canary Islands – Majorca – Minorca – Torremelinos – Benidorm – Fuengirola – Costa Brava – Formentara - Puerto Rico
- Madrid
- Switzerland – Geneva – St Moritz
- Austria – Igls – Innsbruck – Salzburg – Vienna
- Iceland – Reykjavik
- Nepal – Everest – Kathmandu - Lukla
- Doha
- Dubai
- Jersey
- Germany – Berlin – Moenchengladbach – Lippstadt – Krefeld – Lubbecke – Herford – Bertchesgarden – Konigsee – Winterburg – Koln – Dortmund – Kassel – Frankfurt – Hohne – Wildenrath – Schleswig Holstein – Bavaria – Munich – Bielefeld – Black Mountains – Mohnesee – Dusseldorf - Helgoland
- Italy – Cervinina – Milan - Venice – **Got engaged on the Rialto bridge 23/04/2005**
- France – Paris – Boulogne - Calais
- Barcelona
- Madeira – Funchal
- Belgium – Brugge
- Canada – Hamilton – Montreal – Quebec – Ottawa – Toronto – Vancouver & Vancouver Island

- America – Las Vegas – San Francisco – Monterrey – Carmel – San Diego – Santa Barbara – Venice Beach – Palm Springs – Idyllwild – New York – Baltimore – Washington – Philadelphia – Atlantic City – Cape May
- England – Nuneaton – Coventry – Birmingham – Stoke – Lichfield – Atherstone – Tamworth – Manchester – Liverpool – Newcastle – Peak District (all over) – Derby – Leeds – York – Sherburn in Elmet – Lake District – Devon – Cornwall – Somerset – Gloucestershire – Buckinghamshire –Worcestershire – Berkshire – **Lowestoft** – Norwich - Ipswich
- Scotland – Ayrshire – Glasgow – Edinburgh – Aberdeen – Stirling – Fort William
- Wales – Snowdonia – Tenby – Saundersfoot – Cardiff – Swansea – Neath – Pontypridd – Wrexham - Newport
- Cyprus – Paphos – Nicosia – all over the island
- Turkey – Marmaris
- Greece – Rhodes
- Morroco - Marrakech
- Sweden – Malmo
- Holland
- Guernsey – Sark
- Lanzarote

My Only Daughter

Born Kerry Lianne Horobin 05/11/1979. Well given that I split up with her Mother before she was 1 years old (see Chapter VII) it saddens me as to where we are today with our relationship. Now I can hear you all thinking well it takes two, yes you're absolutely right. Two to get it right and two to get it wrong, irrespective if one is more to blame than the other. Sadly in the world as we know it some people never get it right or attempt to put it right. As I have said many times before, once time has passed you can never, repeat never, get it back no matter the occasion or excuse. We have as a race all over this world created sayings to fit every picture and they are affected by many factors in life. Some we live by, others we use to say I told you so and others to fit the current picture. I will not insult anyone's intelligence by listing them all.

So how does one put right the errant ways in which we find ourselves, not a question of whom but how. No matter who puts it right or starts the process it will fail if both parties do not subscribe to it. I have never been a full time parent ever in my life, not necessarily by choice either I can assure you. Always with my daughter I have been an outsider looking in as explained in Chapter VII. Also I wrote a letter when I was 21 years old on exactly what I would miss as a father. I sent it to my mother who gave it to Kerry when she was 18 years old, it would be nice if from time to time she would reflect and read it. Not I may add to judge her own mother but to try and understand how I felt and how I feel to this very day.

Kerry was a typical playful, very energetic child. I had high hopes that she would take after me. In many ways she did, very competitive just like me. The influence I would like to have had was negated by her Mum and me splitting up, the reason why doesn't matter. Now in life we have to have core values, grow up slowly and have fun, complete our education, get a job, pay taxes and be a credit to society. Some of the things now to be written I have never said to Kerry, our relationship as it is would not allow it. Now to that bloody word opinion again, in my opinion Kerry has shown little regard for any of the core values most of us choose, as a society, to live by. Equally to be fair to her mother and partner I do not know if she would be different had she grown up with me. Please note that it is never too late in life to change anything if you wish to do so. Let's not forget I wasted most of my own education whilst at school (big regret). But later in life I hopefully caught up. If Kerry has done more than I currently know then please accept my apologies.

Sorry if this part of my story seems to be all over the place. My writing is very much following my thought processes as they occur with no format to be followed. Which I think in my own mind is essential in the way I am writing this piece.

After my split from Kerry's Mum I chose to give my access to my parents and carry on with my career as a soldier in Germany. This also meant that I could see Kerry as often as allowed and phone her each and every weekend at my Mum and Dad's house only. Kerry's Mum strictly controlled the collections, we were not even allowed to knock on the front door of their house but had to sound the horn upon arrival. More than once in the early days I had an altercation with her Mum's partner over visits. A social worker controlled the first access rights and a court of law told me how much money I had to pay for Kerry's upbringing. I never missed a payment; in fact her Mum was issued with a payment book for Kerry. Her Mum also asked me if I would allow her partner to adopt Kerry as his own daughter, the answer was then and still is now a very firm **NO**. Kerry has however taken to using a different surname to that of mine; after all she is an adult in her own right.

As she got older we took holidays together, however before we could get started I had to take her Mum to court to gain holiday access because of her constant refusal to allow me to take Kerry away. Like most of us not knowing what the future holds I ploughed through life following my sporting dreams. Kerry was always in my thoughts and I told anyone who would listen about my daughter, showing the latest photographs. Any relationship that I had would require my partner to spend time with us (me and Kerry) or it was definitely a non starter. Much to my relief I met some lovely people who were only too happy to share the relationship with us both. On one of my access days I took Kerry to the local Woolworths to obtain a photo. Remember the black and white photo booths, truly revolutionary in those days. I have carried that photo around with me since that day and still carry it today as I write this chapter. I proudly tell all that ask that it is the first photo of me and Kerry after I split up from her Mum. I will keep this photo on me at all times until I die.

The beauty then and today in being a parent is how proud you feel when they are with you and other people see how they are growing up into nice people. God was I gifted in having a very good looking daughter to be with. Although I have not seen her for a while I feel sure she is still the same. Not forgetting that she now has a daughter of her own (Liberty), guess I will not see her either now. Maybe mother time will become the great healer, possibly at the moment too many opinions are at the forefront of this issue.

As a young girl we were like chalk and cheese during my visits, my time was completely hers. When taking her home I used to carry her on my shoulders from Nuneaton to her home in Bedworth. Often listening to the latest rhyme she had learned along with some choice ones as she got older.

As stated above, Kerry like me is very competitive. Once I taught her how to walk on her hands. She practiced until she could walk further than me and I was fairly good. She later became an accomplished gymnast. I still have the videos of her in competition. So, so proud. It is my hope that she did not feel any pressure from me, although Kerry would be better served to answer that question. If we never speak again maybe one day she will read this and come to terms with the way I am thinking. I know she has attempted to study and attended evening classes in psychiatry and law. Hopefully she will achieve all that she wants, becoming a respected member of society as we know it, making all the right choices for herself and her own children. Kerry, from what little I know of her school life, seems to have been a bit like me whilst growing up. Either easily led or trying to be the leader. Whatever scam between school kids was available you could be sure that somewhere I would play my part. On one occasion Kerry and her friends blanked out a copy of a birth certificate, then using the school printer made lots of copies and distributed them to friends. They then wrote in the same details as on their genuine birth certificate just changing the birth year. They even aged the certificate by wrinkling it to make it look like the real thing so that when challenged they could proudly produce it. The only thing is, Kerry is quite small and very, very, annoyingly youthful looking.

My dearest wish is to understand the thought processes of people who choose to live off the state or from illicit gains. How do they live with themselves knowing that how they live affects the lives of innocent and often weaker (socially) people? Is it accepted as a way of living? Surely it is better to be a part of society than against it all the time? What values do they instil in their own children, or do they in turn become the next generation of spongers? No I am not naïve and I am appreciative of the social status of this world and how it is not always fair. But again, like my parents wanted for us, surely all you want is for your children to grow up and work their way through life. Hopefully being successful and contributing to society.

I'm not after thanks from Kerry but an appreciation of how I have tried to help her would have been nice. Even when it was financial it was thrown back in my face so whilst continual thanks is not needed, some appreciation is. Since I left school I have worked continually, what I could afford I had and what I could not afford I could not have (that simple). Earlier I mentioned the three types of people who make up the world in a book called 'How to be Happy Though Human', 1. Turnip, 2. Artist and 3. Businessman. Which one do you think this is? It's a very good book to both read and understand and was written in 1932, reprinted by W. Beran Wolfe M.D. Some people seem born to take all and give nothing in return. Again I feel duty bound to say that this is only my opinion of the situation. I was always Kerry's best friend and Dad when something was wanted or needed. And usually I was able to help as I have always been careful and good with money.

You're probably thinking that all I am doing is moan about the situation. Well sadly this has been building for years in many ways. Private conversations have been had on many occasions. Put simply though we are who we are. Kerry was, and almost certainly still is, a loving person; she is certainly a very good Mum herself. As a child she was fantastic and had no control over how I and her Mum dealt with our situation. My only bad thing to say about her Mum is that she has, again in my own opinion, got it sadly wrong. As the years passed so much more could have been done to allow us to interact for our daughter's sake. This was most definitely not forthcoming but that question needs to be asked of her mother and partner.

Memories and thoughts of growing up with Kerry, albeit from a distance are too numerous to mention. On a holiday to Minorca the local waiter took a shine to her but he had no chance because of me. I followed them everywhere even to a nightclub (she was only 16 and a rebel), Kerry tried desperately to get time alone with him. She will find out exactly what I was doing when her own daughter comes of age and she realises that all he wanted was his wicked way. Not a bloody chance whilst I was on patrol matey. I once woke her up in Germany at 05:00 to take her running with my running club (6 miles). Not only did she run it but at the end finished she the run doing backwards flick flaks (gymnastics) to great applause. I let her lie in for the rest of the holiday after that. We went on long outings on my motorbike, travelling all over Germany. At Ace's (also in Germany) she outlasted all three brothers through an all night drinking session and sang along to all the records that we played.

Kerry has had an up and down relationship with the father of her daughter, they have tried to live together and failed. Deep down I believe that he cares for her but they are not suited together as a couple. He is though as far as I know a very good and responsible father, as I was to Kerry. My daughter has not created a barrier between him and his daughter as her own Mum created for me. They both have a lot to learn especially about the definition of the word **INFIDELITY**. Not only about what it means but also what it does, and will continue to do, to families throughout this world. After all it was the reason why me and her Mum split up.

Her partner has been to jail twice and I know that the situation has caused conflict between Kerry and her mother to the point where they did not speak for a while. Whilst her partner was in prison Kerry visited him frequently so he could see their daughter, very commendable. (It's a pity her own mother didn't put Kerry first when we split up.) Through them chatting he asked for a second chance with Kerry, which she agreed to. This caused massive disruption with her own mother so she sought my opinion. I gave them both my support, whether they were going to work as a couple or not was not down to me. They themselves had to put in the hard work any relationship needs to survive and exist. Initially they were close but sadly it ended in failure, but at least they tried. Who knows where in the relationship world Kerry is headed, we all deserve love and happiness because it makes you feel good. Whatever circles and influences she has now surrounded herself with I assume will suffice. I would like a chance to talk with her but am equally not sure that I would get through to her. The company that she keeps (not all) seem happy to sponge their way through life taking and giving nothing in return. Everyone values love, happiness, comfort etc. differently.

So where are we headed or what could or can be done to make things different? In order to resolve the situation and hit a happy medium how do we get round this? One of us needs to start with **"do you know what; I am not always right and am willing to compromise my thoughts, views and opinions in**

order to save and hold onto this relationship". Can it be changed? Are these fruitless exchanges of words, sayings or meanings? As each day passes by it becomes harder to undo, who makes the first move? If however each party considers this is it and no matter how hard we try our differences cannot be overcome then let's get on with life. Without, and I mean, without being judgemental, perhaps you are laughing at that comment. We create so many words to overcome all eventualities that we forget the people involved. Not forgetting a solid friend will always tell you that you are right. A question I would like an answer to is what she really meant when she said to someone **"I hate my Dad",** I've attempted to cover all angles here:

- I said it in the heat of the moment!
- I did not mean it I was angry!
- I did mean it!

Should be enough but the list could go on: My Dad would say keep it simple so I have tried. For my part I would dearly love to be part of Kerry and Liberty's lives but, and there always has to be a bloody but, perhaps the damage was done long ago. We did not always seem to see eye to eye so it could be for the best; Even after this has been written it will happen to other families and will continue to do so throughout life sadly. We are in a world where we seek a reason for everything. My thoughts right now are not to continue seeking but to get on with my life. I will not entertain accusations of being spendthrift, going on holidays, etc. All that I have done and have achieved has been through going to work everyday of my life so far. The same cannot be said about Kerry in return. I do not owe anyone a penny and have never even owned a credit card. As my Mum would say, "if you can afford it you can have it and if you cannot afford then you can't". As I said before I was not questioned when I provided help in whatever form to Kerry.

I think before I lose track that whether it is believed or not I do really **LOVE** Kerry and wished it could be easier. Maybe it will never change and it will eventually be too late to alter our course. Perhaps the first time Kerry will know my feelings will be when, or if, she reads this book. If that is the case then it will mean that I will never know her side of the story. Perhaps when we all get to the other side of life we will all become friends and wonder why we wasted so much time.

For the sceptics or judgemental people who may be reading this, below is a copy of a letter (albeit a brief one) that I delivered to my daughter's flat on 03/09/2008. One thing I do not know however is if she still lives at this address in Bedworth, although it all looked familiar. (I could be wrong)

Kerry & Liberty

Hello to you both, unless one of us tries to end this distance between us then we will miss out on a lot of things I guess. That said if we are to spend time in each others lives then we both need to put an end to this.

I have thought about you both a lot and had many a conversation about you, but it is not the same as seeing you in person (I don't mean every day before you get worried!) I have sent messages to the mobile numbers I have with your name but assume you no longer have them. I have also called your flat phone which is no longer recognised. If you no longer live there then I am truly stuffed.

If you would like to meet when you're ready please let me know, let's see if we can come to some kind of understanding before it's too late.

You can contact me on **077******03**.

However if you wish the situation to remain the same then I sincerely wish you both well and all that occurs in your lives.

Dad & GranDad XXX

I'm now a very little user of the modern day communications called Facebook. My daughter is a member, and another family member saw her on Facebook with a different surname to mine. On her page she is named as Kerry Budworth which is the name of her mother's husband. I was told this sometime in 2009. Not sure whether she has changed her name by deed poll or just out of choice. Not even sure why I am writing this, probably a little upset I guess. Still being an adult it is her choice what name she goes by.

Sadly Kerry's Mum denied me being a Father and now Kerry herself is denying me being a Grandfather.

My little lady Kerry

My (bigger) little lady Kerry with my Granddaughter Liberty

Chapter VII

Relationships/Marriage/Divorce/Sex

Well how to sum this chapter up in a meaningful and pleasant way, suffice to say that I have had more than my fair share of ups and downs. Sadly in today's world we seem to have become an **"if it don't work, then don't fix it culture, so replace it instead"**. This seems to be aimed as much at relationships as the normal, everyday products that we buy.

Anyway before we go into that statement lets ascertain what exactly do we learn as we grow up about relationships. Well I suppose the first people we see in a relationship are our parents. Some, and hopefully, most parents make a great and long lasting go of things, therefore inspiring their children with the same ideals. Sadly as we know some parents get it horrendously wrong giving off a tainted view of relationships which children carry into their very own lives.

My parents were, I thought, happy for many years but I think they wore each other down towards the end. No matter that though because my own personal belief about relationships is as true to my upbringing today measured against the failures which I will talk about. My belief was that I would meet a woman, fall in love, get married and have a family. Thankfully this still occurs in society today but it is becoming increasingly rare. Reasons as to why relationships fail is a book all on its own, which probably needs to be written by someone with more time and alleged knowledge than me. What upsets me is, no matter whether it's a celebrity or mainstream relationship that goes wrong, the desire to slate the other person always seems to be there. I have some bad views on break ups as well but let's not also forget that I did fall in love with these people and them with me. Not forgetting that they too have a point of view on the break up.

I got off to a good start, met a girl, fell in love and got her pregnant (not planned!). What I will say is that I hope I have been fair in my explanation of the story but leave the rest up to you. So the first point could always be that we were too young, 18 and 16 respectively. All of a sudden I was being pressured to get married, something I did not want to do until after our baby was born. Eventually I gave in and we got married, it was the right thing to do apparently. We were given a council house and with great help from both families we moved in. We decorated and bought second hand furniture and appliances, it was very neat considering the speed it was completed in, due to the baby's arrival. Our daughter (Kerry Lianne Horobin) was born on 05/11/1979 and my god she was beautiful. Not long after she was born I lost my job (that temper again!) and decided to join the Army, which meant us being separated whilst I completed my training. This next bit needs to be mentioned for what it's worth. My wife's (Rita) Mum did not care for me much and in my opinion became the main instigator in breaking us up. Of course you have never heard that one before have you? Equally I have never had the chance to tell my daughter. Mainly because we are estranged.

So off I went to join the Army, signing up for 9 years as security for myself and my new family. During my trade training in Catterick we were allocated to army quarters and lived there with our new dog Ben as a family. Everything was tight with regard to money and living but as far as I knew all was well between us. Once I was posted to Germany Rita went to live with her parents whilst we waited for a house to be allocated to us overseas. In those days you did not get an automatic allocation. Rita and Kerry accompanied me to Trent Valley station in Nuneaton to see me off on the train to Brize Norton to catch a plane to Germany. I remember it vividly to this day, waving to them both through the window upstairs looking out to the front of the station. The very same window still makes my heart pang today.

I received numerous letters declaring how much I was loved by my wife, equally how much they both missed me. After completing basic and trade training I was posted to Germany where I quickly put our name down and waited for a house to be allocated. After 3 months of waiting we got a house, as soon as I was given the address I phoned my wife in England who in less than one minute of talking announced that she was leaving me and not coming. The phone was put down and no one would answer my further calls. The Army allowed me compassionate leave to go home, to try and sort things out. Upon my arrival they (Rita and Kerry) had gone into hiding, I was the Mafia all of a sudden! Well I found them pretty quickly and like a madman picked up our daughter and ran, talk about World War three! I have never seen so many police in my life, they caught me at my mother's house. Obviously I gave her back and to be fair they understood that I was upset. My wife was now with another man, someone I later found out she had been seeing since I had left for the Army. To be fair to them they are still together to this day. They had sold all the contents of our house and spent the money on holidays. The hurt that I personally felt and have always felt when a relationship ends is absolutely horrendous. So my idea of a relationship between two people was shattered by my very first experience of it. It was to be 8 long years before I allowed anyone special into my life again. Your confidence is knocked for a while afterwards but one has to try again. **Surely it could not happen twice**.

Soon after we split we were led into the path of the good old social worker to arrange visitation rights (an idea pinched from America!). I felt like I was the biggest monster on the planet. Having no idea what my ex-partner had told the social worker about me, thankfully she was quite fair. It was hit and miss over the next months whether my ex would let me have our daughter or not. Often I was turned away empty-handed from a planned visit so it became clear that we would have to go to court. Again I was painted as the partner and father from hell, was I really this person? The judge was pretty fair in that he gave me weekend access and I was to pay for our daughter each month. This I gladly did until she was sixteen, along with all the other things which were more costly. The sad side to the court hearing was that I was arrested and subsequently bound over to keep the peace for one year. My ex and her new fellow turned up to court with his mates and decided to attack me in the toilets. They were in for a very big shock, my retaliation set them running. Nothing to be proud of I may add (that temper again) but I was out of control after they hit me. I said we had rights in an earlier sentence, what I meant was, is that my Mum and Dad were given access as well (the first Grandparents to receive this, something Mum was very proud of). I, or mostly Mum, picked Kerry up throughout her life every Saturday without fail. We were not allowed to knock on the door at anytime, we tooted the car horn and she was sent out. A situation which never changed throughout all the years. Now you would think that as the years passed of us not being together that we could, for the common goal of our daughter, cease hostilities. Sadly this was and, to this day, never has been the case. When our daughter was

146

having a tough time Kerry contacted me and asked me to talk to her Mum. Kerry gave me a phone number to ring but as soon as I introduced myself I was told never to ring this number again. That after almost 13 years of separation, not to worry though because I feel totally sure my point will be refuted. I don't suppose that our daughter has ever been told that they wanted me to sign her over for adoption. Not a chance, I totally refused to cooperate on this matter. She was mine and that's the way it will remain, even though these days we do not have a relationship to speak of.

During the next 8 years I met various ladies, some I liked more than others but none special enough to commit to. Having said that though there was one young lady who loved me to death and before I realised I felt the same about her it was too late as I had already done too much damage to the relationship. I hope to meet her again one day so I can truly look her in the eye and apologise for my behaviour. I sincerely hope she is happy. During the 8 years I did however get engaged once and must make a mention of another lady whom I think about all the time.

I met a lady through a pen pal agency, corresponded with her and when I finally met her instantly fell in love. So I gathered did she, we corresponded regularly and met as often as we could. Approaching our first Christmas after getting engaged she announced that she would like a trial separation. Upon asking why and not receiving the best explanation I decided to agree. She never saw me again: The only devastation I felt after was losing the friendship I had gained with her mother.

So picking myself up again I marched on, after training in England at Haringey Athletics Club (in the 1980s) we were on a bus back to Germany. It was decided we would stop off for a break in Maidstone.

We chose the pub only because a sign said 'Wet T-Shirt' competition. It had finished as we arrived but one of the barmaids was still wearing her wet t-shirt. Bingo we were like wow, how nice was she with lovely assets on display through the t-shirt. Well it was me who impressed her enough to swap numbers and addresses. All the way back to Germany I was attacked for this information, but I did not give it to anyone. A wonderful correspondence started and we became lovers shortly after. I visited as often as I could; she was the most outward, vivacious person you could wish to meet. So full of life, always happy and willing to try anything. Absolutely all that you could wish for in life, sadly though we lost touch as we struggled with the distance. A year or so later I was posted back to England and decided to contact her again. She replied and said she would like to meet but also to tell me things had changed. She would tell me more when we met. Now being honest I was thinking we would carry on almost where we left off. We agreed to meet after I had finished some winter bobsleigh training at Thorpe Park in London. I booked the hotel and smiled inwardly of what was to come (fingers crossed). As I walked towards her don't ask me how but I knew something was wrong. She was hardly recognisable as the same person I first met and fell in love with. Well we booked into the hotel and sat down to what at first felt like a forced conversation. She confided in me that she had, a short while ago, been attacked. The conversation stopped dead, how do I respond? I wanted to hold and hug her, but even that I felt I ought not to do. Where had the bubbly, effervescent character that I first met gone? She was half the bodyweight she used to be and god did she look gaunt. No life in her eyes, such a contrast to the person I knew when we first met. My instincts said offer to kill the bastard that committed the attack, but I did not. I did give her a warm hug and hoped it was enough. We had a meal that evening and when we retired to bed I slept on the chair not wishing to upset or offend her. Now I am not an expert on women being attacked, all I can tell you is that it destroyed this person. Somehow though life has to be restored, my only hope is that what we discussed was enough for her. Three years later I met my second wife, the weekend before the wedding I was at my Mum's sorting out last minute details. Mum said 'Dean, I have received a phone call from (MK)' which was her correct name. She had looked in the phonebook for my surname and phoned all numbers until she had found me. Mum innocently told her I was getting married to which she offered her congratulations. But she told Mum please tell Dean I am ok and now have a little daughter and a loving man. It's a wonderful outcome and I often think about her to this very day. I have told my current wife (you've guessed now, I've been married 3 times).

I got married for the second time in 1989 to a girl I met in the Army in York. Everyone thought that she was a plain Jane type of girl but I saw through that, our deep conversations, as friends at first, led me to warm to her and subsequently fall in love with her. She was from Leeds and a very down to earth girl (or so I thought). Our relationship went from friends to lovers to marriage, our family values were so alike, surely this must be a match made in heaven. We had a common love of sport at a high level, both competitive and both still active in competition. We were together for 13 years and married for 11, sadly though upon reflection we should have split up after the first two years. I have added that early on because if only I as a person was less loyal I would have walked away. If she had not walked away I would still have been in a bad relationship today, for that I applaud her. Her family were lovely non-judgemental people and I continued to see her GrandDad and take him on holidays long after we split up, he is now 87 years young. To be fair I believe that we fell in love for all the right reasons but when two people go through life together you have to want to be a part of each other's changes. Because of her job, which meant she went away for days and weeks at a time, we grew apart. We did not have to, but when one of the partner's stops giving to the other then you have a problem. I do not wish to do her a disservice and explain issues within the relationship because bitterness clouds judgement and as I said at the beginning we fell in love with each other once. Suffice to say that major parts in a relationship which should be important to each individual were very sadly lacking. We had a trial separation in the late 1990s, perhaps then we should have let go. What is ironic is that before we split up we bought a house and spent £20,000 renovating it, she left just after we moved in. I delivered all her belongings to her parent's house and after delivering the last load I thanked her Dad for allowing me to marry his daughter. Sadly as well as my first marriage other parties were involved as I found out by reading email after she left. I do not make a habit of reading my partner's email by the way, they were left on the computer when she left, she forgot to delete these ones although many other things were deleted. I have all the luck I guess.

The marriage ended in 2000, so I drifted through life hurt again but not despondent. I had a relationship with someone from my home town who wanted to keep it a secret from her family. This I honoured but never understood, and then I met someone from work who proceeded to turn my life upside down for the next 3.5years. Sadly someone else was involved again, a so called friend who took offence when I punched him on the nose. The relationship cost me a lot of money and I allowed it to happen, what I miss though is her little son whom I took into my life and miss dearly to this day. Throughout the relationship it was a constant battle to keep up with her emotions, paying for her son's education, childcare and all the household bills whilst they lived with me. And yes I do mean all the bills which included paying off some of her debts. Was I soft you shout? Probably yes, however return should not be measured against outlay unless you have problems and boy did we have problems. She was even seeing someone else at our workplace where we met when I first met her. This she kept quiet until it all came out, I should have run away then.

So back on my own again, my younger brother was brilliant here, every day I called upon him usually late at night to go for a coffee. He never once let me down and not forgetting that he had a family of his own. Also a big thanks to his partner Cat. After a while he suggested that I go onto the Internet and sign up to a dating agency. Around this time I also took the decision to stop drinking altogether. A dating agency? Never, it's surely a knocking shop and nothing more. What it is, in today's world, is a way of corresponding and getting to know someone long before meeting stage. No different to going out and meeting someone, you still have to decide whether to pursue it or not. So I registered with Friends Reunited, completed a profile, looked at the ladies and sent some requests off. Having logged on I was surprised at just how many people were on it. I looked in an area within 25 miles of my home town. I must admit at being frustrated, thinking that I would get replies daily. This did not happen, however after about a week I got some replies, living in Nuneaton my field of search was not that wide. One lady 8 miles away corresponded for a while but she decided that the distance between us was too much to overcome. Another lady said because I had a child it was not possible, my retort was that at that time my daughter was 25 years old and did not even live with me. I never met anyone in those first three months so I decided to broaden my search area up to 200 miles, off went the contacts and I waited.

The following deserves its own paragraph: One of my messages went to a lady from Lowestoft (160 miles away) known only as **MAIDMAZ**. Allow me to add that my profile request for a woman was that she must be under 40 and have a lovely bottom or I would not pursue it. Please don't judge me but it is the particular part of the female anatomy that I like. Shock horror she replied, we swapped a few emails giving snippets of our lives. In December of 2004 I was racing in Wales on Mount Snowdon, having told Marion (MAIDMAZ) of my plans she texted me to ask how I had got on. My reply was that I would explain all if she was offering to cook me a Sunday lunch, the race was on the Saturday. Marion suggested that we meet for the first time halfway between where we both lived and have that lunch. We were to meet at 15:00hrs in the Tesco car park in Newmarket on 19/12/2004. I arrived early very nervous, as 15:00 came and went I thought I had been stood up, however at 15:10 I spotted her car (MR2, Silver). Marion still contests to this day that it was I who was late. Anyway as she got out of the car I had a sneaky look at her figure and was mightily impressed. Well we parked up and walked into town looking for somewhere to talk first and eat later. Now come on here, it is my belief that when you meet someone whom excites you physically and mentally in such an overwhelming way you just know that feeling. Bang, it hit me straight away and at 22:30 that night we were struggling to part. We talked for hours and had many laughs along the way, had a sumptuous meal (we returned to the same hotel on our 1st year anniversary as a couple and stayed the night in a four poster bedroom). Before we parted I invited Marion to come with me to Edinburgh for a three day pre-Christmas break in four days. Her friends thought she was mad but she accepted my offer later that first night. Our feet have not touched the ground ever since. We had two small confessions to get out at our first meeting. Marion was really 42 and not 40 and I had given her my work mobile number. Marion had also asked if I had checked out her bottom to which I replied yes within the first 10 seconds. I also need to add that whilst in Newmarket I found a penny on the floor, which I picked up for luck and we have it today in a special box in our house.

Marion had been in a relationship for 23 years with a guy called Andy and they had split up four years before we met. The reason why I mention this is because when we first met Marion said in almost the first sentence " I am bossy and friends with my Ex, if you have a problem with either of these things then we have a problem" talk about forward. I visited Marion after our trip to Edinburgh in Lowestoft and went to her local for New Years Eve. I met this fantastic bloke who made me, a total stranger, so welcome. At the end of the evening I asked Marion who it was and she replied that's my Ex. Now hold on a minute Marion was not ignorant by way of introduction, the night though went so fast we never got round to introducing everyone. Today as we speak he has become a friend, albeit mainly to Marion, we ourselves get along just fine. In fact we have been out with him numerous times on visits. It also turns out that a previous boyfriend of Marion's gave Andy and Marion a hard time over their friendship. I however live in the real world I hope.

Well we (Marion and I) agreed to see each other every other weekend initially because of the 160 miles between us. However as I said in the paragraph above, when you meet someone special the feeling is overwhelming. Every other week became every weekend and also on a Wednesday night each week. This was so real, my company car clocked up over 150,000 miles with work and visiting Marion in just over two years (got a new one now). Our relationship went from strength to strength: **Marion is the only woman I have taken to meet my MUM whereby my Mum said on the very first visit I like her**. Shock horror, Mum was always unresponsive initially but with Marion it was different. My Dad also liked Marion very much, so clean he commented, a feature my Mum also liked. In February 2005 we flew to Berlin for Marion's birthday, too cold for Marion but a lovely place. So in April I booked a romantic visit to Venice, in Mum's kitchen I told her that this was real and do you think it's too early to ask for Marion's hand in marriage. After all it was only just over four months down the line, the support I was given was unreal. Question now was where would I propose? On a Gondola stood out, so that's where the request would be made. I did the gentlemanly thing and asked Marion's Mum for her hand in marriage: Sadly Marion's father is no longer with us and had died before I met her. We arrived in Venice and it was my intention to ask Marion to marry me on the gondola on 23/04/2005. I thought let's get this out of the way first thing and enjoy the rest of the day. I hid the ring in my pocket and would not let Marion near my left hand side so she would not detect it. Well whilst on the gondola I could not, repeat could not, get the words out. The ride finished and I had not proposed, so what now. We walked round Venice all through the day and I was searching for a moment to propose. We stood on the Rialto Bridge when, at 18:00 the bells from the church sounded. Talk about the moment, looking at Marion I asked her what she would say if I asked her to marry me (not as romantic as I wanted to make it). Marion replied that she would say yes, so thereafter I asked her and we became engaged. It turned out to be appropriate, both in location and timing in many ways (more why later). I took Marion back to our room where I opened for her a small bottle of champagne which I had brought across and a bottle of coke for me . We still have the cork from the bottle at our home. What a fantastic holiday it was, it also turned out that Marion's friends were expecting me to propose (how did they know or guess?), the signs must have been obvious.

So now we were engaged and so many plans had to be made. Rightly or wrongly it was assumed by everyone that I would move to Lowestoft to live. I had lived anywhere but my home town all my working life since leaving school. I had moved back to my home town purely because my house was cheaper than my room in London, where I was working and still work today. Marion however decided that for the first time in her life maybe she would like to move. In November 2005 Marion moved to my house in Nuneaton after selling hers in Lowestoft. My house was also up for sale as we wanted to both start anew in our very own home. Whilst waiting for mine to sell we started the absolutely frustrating process of searching for a new one. We looked all over Warwickshire, we did see some wonderful homes but something was missing in each one. Getting close to having to move we found a home which fitted our needs and budget. Placing a deposit on the house, then my house sale fell through. Now we had two mortgages to pay for a while and we all want that don't we?! One thing was becoming clearer now in my life and that was just how practical and determined Marion actually was and is. Making it abundantly clear how we could afford it and that we should forge ahead. A trait that I admire in her to this day as further entries in this chapter will testify. In December 2005 excitedly we moved into our new home, it did not tick all the boxes but it was ours.

The wedding plans were also moving along at great speed, we set a date of 23/04/2006. Those who have read the above closely should have noticed that it was a year to the day since our engagement. So where were we to wed I hear you asking? As a joke very early in our relationship I told Marion that I would marry her in Las Vegas. Marion being Marion found a hotel in Las Vegas called the **VENETIAN**. Look it up on any website and be amazed, not only is it fantastic it is a re-creation of Venice. Not only that, they held wedding ceremonies on their version of the Rialto Bridge in the hotel. This was built indoors over a river, just like the real thing where we had become engaged. Marion planned not only the wedding but also our honeymoon trip around California taking in the sites. My good lady should do this as a business, not only much cheaper than here in England but very exciting. Our wedding, honeymoon, car hire, hotels, wedding apparel and the party back home cost less than £5,000. Believe me when I tell you we lived like King and Queen. No hotel was under 4 star and we travelled all over California over the 2 weeks we were there. Marion's Mum came along with us for the wedding. She had never even flown before so we also took her for a helicopter trip over the Grand Canyon, which was one of her ambitions, killing two birds with one stone. Marion has friends based in California who came to Vegas to help us celebrate our very special day, we also met up with them later in the next week in Santa Barbara.

A reception was held in Lowestoft when we returned so we could celebrate with all our family and friends who could not make it to the actual wedding. Marion's Mum flew home after four days and we in our hire car toured California.

San Francisco: We drove to San Francisco from Las Vegas totally underestimating the time and distance so we had an unscheduled stopover in a place called **Fresno**. I'm sure it is a nice place but for us it should have been called oh no, sorry if I cause any offence to people living there. **San Francisco** is a beautiful city and we just had to visit Alcatraz. What a story to be told visiting here. Two days later we followed Route 1 along the coast taking in **Monterrey** and **Carmel**. Both are truly stunning places. Clint Eastwood lives in Carmel although we were not invited for tea. Anyone wishing to visit the state of California should start at the top and work down the map, that way you keep the sea always on the right hand side of your left hand drive car. Picturesque and totally stunning views from all the vista stops dotted down this famous route. Los Angeles, Santa Barbara and San Diego were all visited, at every hotel I was able to upgrade to the honeymoon suite having told them that we had just got married. I will briefly explain each stop:

Los Angeles: Although it was a nice place we left a little disappointed after seeing it for real as opposed to the pictures one sees on TV during Oscar nights. Other than a small strip and Rodeo drive it is somewhat shabby in appearance. Obviously TV makes it look a lot better. It's sad today that celebrities can buy a star on the pavement as opposed to actually being awarded one, as they used to. The best stars for me were the ones of my favourite TV stars of yesteryear by the late Sid Graumann theatre. John Wayne, Abbott & Costello, Laurel & Hardy and the Keystone Cops. Still in all fairness it brings some people their dreams and shatters others. The obscenity of Rodeo Drive beggars belief, still it's all theirs and as long as they are happy good luck to them, (sorry not a fan of the super rich).

Santa Barbara: What an absolutely stunning place to visit, beaches to die for and so clean. Individual shops to visit, wonderful restaurants and stunning scenery to view and admire. Lots of activities to be had here, depends on just how bold you are in participation.

San Diego: We stayed at a place called Mission Beach just on the edge of San Diego in a harbour fronted by a lake with access to the sea itself. Here I upgraded us to the honeymoon suite having befriended the guy on reception. Mission Bay is fantastic, we had a sea view room with balcony and the bed alone was almost 18ft wide. Jacuzzi bath and stunning furniture finished the room off to a very high standard. Walking around the perimeter in the warm evening sunshine was a treat not to be missed. We visited **Coronado** and the famous hotel (made out of wood) where all the stars and many American presidents have stayed. **La Jolla** is a place to be if you are stinking rich and well worth a visit. The place is littered with money; shops exclusive and very expensive (just like Rodeo Drive in LA). Now then, to anyone who may be reading my thoughts I would like to say please go yourself and make up your own mind. It is my belief that you will not come back disappointed from a trip to anywhere in the state of California. San Diego itself is a beautiful haven, full of fancy restaurants of a very high standard at very affordable budgets. Everyone is treated like King and Queen. They have a shopping Mall called Fashion Valley; I swear it is bigger than the whole town I was born in. It was huge, name a shop and you will find it there with more beside. The location of San Diego alone will leave you breathless if not speechless. I know from my limited explanation that we haven't even scratched the surface yet. And yes, we have been back again visiting even more places for our 1st anniversary. I have deliberately tried to keep my explanations short so as to leave you with plenty to explore if you ever go there. You don't need me or a book to tell you everything, it's for you to discover. It certainly opened up our eyes and we hope to go back again.

The places that we added on our second visit (1st year anniversary 2007) were **Palm Springs** and **Solvang**.

We finished off our trip with a further stay in Las Vegas, again at the hotel Venetian, now unless you have already been to America you won't believe the way they look after you, it is amazing. Nothing is ever too much trouble. Every hotel is a myriad of workers whose purpose is to ensure that you have a great stay. You would have to go some not to enjoy it or enthuse about it afterwards. We were looked after by an appointed wedding adviser (**Angela Cooper**) for our marriage. The whole event was seamless; Angela could not have made it anymore perfect than it was. We have remained friends with Angela and she stayed with us here in England in December 2007. We fully intend to visit her again and regularly keep in touch with her by email.

As mentioned earlier we returned to California for our 1st year anniversary and again stayed in the Hotel Venetian, this time in the Venezia Tower. Once again we hired a car and decided to travel and visit our good friends Ron and Lupe who live in a place called Oxnard which has a lot of very big houses. Well obviously we stayed with Ron and Lupe, in what they called a small house. It makes our houses look tiny! Whilst there we went to a local restaurant (Red Lobster) they knew and had fun with the very young waitress. She loved myself and Marion because of our accents and whilst talking to her we discovered she was working whilst studying to be an opera singer. We teased her a little as she had recently been in a competition where she had come second. If she was only to sing to us we declared she would surely come first, my did she not only sing with such a powerful voice from one so small but the restaurant came to a standstill. And yes she did come first.

We also visited Santa Barbara and me and Ron hired two Segways and had a great time racing up and down the beach paths. Great fun, sadly missed by the ladies because Lupe suffers from motion sickness.

Palm Springs (2007): We added this wonderful town to our list of must go to places, wow sums it up and some. The hotel was sumptuous beyond belief and it was very hot, so much so that as you walked down the main street little spray jets showered you (very lightly) with water to cool you down. If you like steak Palm Springs will take some beating.

Solvang: Apparently some years ago Danish settlers settled in California and built their very own village in the same style as if they were back home in Denmark. This is a not to be missed place if ever you visit California, picturesque and stunning beyond belief.

Venice Beach: Yes the muscle beach does exist, just like in all the body building videos, it's a nice place but much smaller than I imagined. I guess they sought the climate which is very good. The area seemed a little tacky to me and in need of renovation. Our claim to fame was that we dined in the same restaurant as Governor Schwarzenegger (we were inside first I may add).

For me America is certainly a nice place and we have only visited a small portion of it, we hope to cover more in the future. The whole experience from the people to the country itself was, for us, beyond words we can express. They are friendly, warm, helpful, co-operative and really make you feel like you are on holiday.

Back to my lady Marion, this lady makes me feel for the first time a full part of a relationship. The little things she does without announcement are the ones that tickle me the most. It also makes me feel special in her world, nothing she does for me or us is too little. Her calmness and understanding of how I, Dean the person, work deserves a medal all on its own. Mum always said (to Marion as well) that Dean needs a strong woman. I have got it! Now it would be easy to say that I saved the best until last or that God did. I personally think that I had to go through life and learn and constantly change to become the person that I am now. It's wrong to evaluate lots of relationships but equally it's true that you adapt and change things from one encounter to the next. With my Marion we were both upfront from the beginning about our own needs from a relationship. From our often deep conversations we were able to see that each could supply what the other needed. Any slight or very minor issues would be ironed out along the way. We have both had relationships which we entered with the best of intentions. Now it's our turn, rest assured I will give 150,000,000% of effort to what

I consider the last major relationship that I will have in my life.

Plaudits are a plenty when I think of the time that Marion has been part of my life, apart from the fact that she is beautiful. I sometimes err but the fix is usually quicker than the action. The desire to keep things on an even keel is with me at all times throughout every day. As a person, I have never been so relaxed within a relationship and this is absolutely the first time that I have felt equal within it. We live for each other; the common things that should be done are completed with serenity and ease. The small things such as, a thank you after a compliment or a lovely weekend. Opening the car door or any shop door, ensuring that Marion walks on the inside of the path when out, no matter how many times we cross the road.

It is now 6 years since we got married, we recently celebrated 8 years of meeting each other in Newmarket on 19/12/2012. Life is never dull and is lived at some pace, we've just taken our latest trip to Madrid and hope to get back to Las Vegas in 2013 for our 7th wedding anniversary.

We also spend time on our house which, along with our beautiful garden, changes every year. We enjoy growing vegetables and are happy to be able to offer produce from our garden to our neighbours and friends, which is always gratefully received by them.

My beautiful wife Marion (Rhodes in 2005)

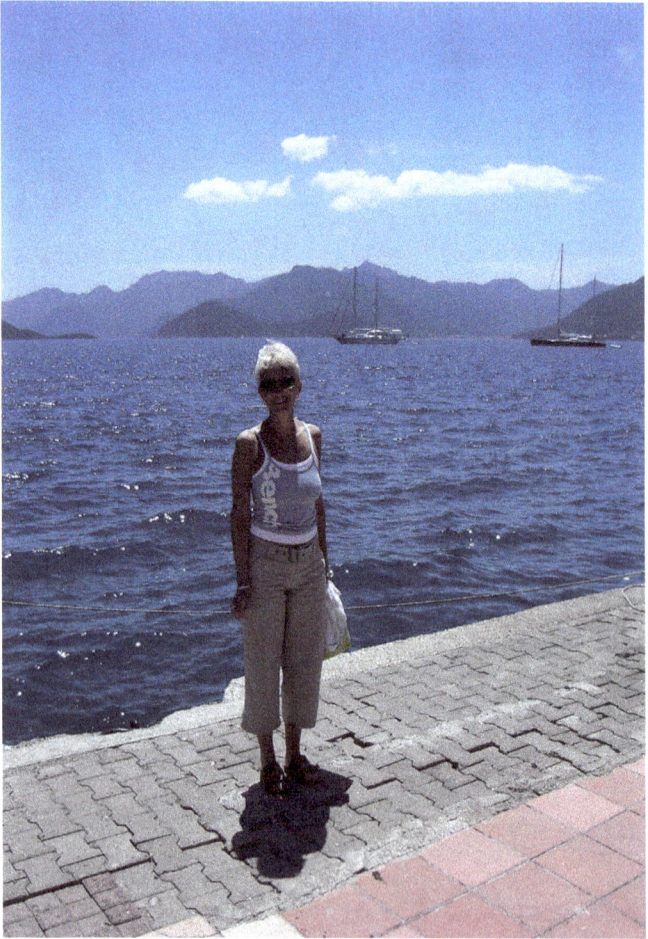

Marion (Marmaris 2005)

Chapter VIII

The Great Outdoors & <u>EVEREST</u>

Before I get onto the subject of Everest allow me to digress and explain just how I became a great lover of the outdoors and the peace and tranquillity that I personally find there.

As a teenager Mum saved up some money to send me on a trip to Wales with my school. We were going to a place called Snowdonia and staying in a youth hostel called Penny Pass, at the base of a mountain called Mount Snowdon. Well it sounded exciting, having only ever been to Skegness this seemed like a trip to the far side of the planet. As the school bus started its journey along the route to Llanberis (I know the name now!) I was taken in by the absolutely stunning scenery on route to our destination. Like a schoolboy lost, whatever occurred that day and throughout the trip made me want more. The terrain amazed me, coming from a town I did not then know that so much space existed. It was rugged, high, low and colourful with sheep, buildings, mines and hardy people, just some of the things I took in and enjoyed as I have over the years since that day. The hostel was a blast but for me the best was climbing the mountain. We took the Miners Track route up and down that first day, the lakes, the mines, the black and white pictures in the café. All had to be taken in and remembered, when I return these days I tell all who will listen about the routes I climbed. I have, on many occasions since that first time taken my friends to share and enjoy what I see. Now all has changed at the base and at the top of Snowdon, a new cafe on top and a re-vamp at the bottom cafe.

Suffice to say that I have spent many days in and around Snowdonia since that first visit and to this day I climb my beloved Mount Snowdon at least 10 times each year. Indeed when it is my time to leave this earth it is my wish that my ashes are scattered from the summit of Mount Snowdon. Then if life after death does exist my first awakening will be surrounded by all the beauty and serenity one gets each and every time you climb that mountain. The routes are many, Miners Track, Pyg Track, Llanberis, Crib Goch and each has its own beauty.

I think it's difficult to explain to anyone reading this just how one feels when walking no matter where it takes place or which country it is in. My thinking these days is that it's personal to the individual and whilst it should be shared if warranted or requested it's probably best left that way. Other far more competent writers have said it all, I would urge you to read anything by the late Mr Wainwright. His books are full of wonderful explanations.

Over the years I have travelled extensively to walk, run or climb mountains as well as taking in so many breath-taking sights along the way. I'm lucky enough to have been able to visit the Lake District, the Peak District, the Malverns, Snowdonia, Brecon Beacons, Scotland, the Black Mountains in Germany, the Atlas Mountains in Morocco, Italy, Switzerland, Austria and many more. The freedom, isolation and at times feelings of danger always lead to a fantastic experience. With any luck I will have many, many more years to come where I can continue to enjoy all the feelings gained so far from being outside.

Well as the world gets smaller and dreams become more obtainable the thought of going to Nepal and seeing Everest became a reality. Along with my Uncle

David (Dad's youngest brother) we decided to book the trip of a lifetime.

I have got to confess at this point that if I can ever raise sufficient money I would love to make a summit attempt.

Until then allow me to share my experience with you. To be fair David took care of all the fine details such as which company to travel with and flights, etc. The trip was booked using a company called Safe Journeys, based in Scotland, who came highly recommended. In fact such was the calibre of the company the founder (Richard) organised a pre-trip get together in Scotland for all team members to meet. Unfortunately I could not make it to Scotland so I eventually met up with my fellow travellers at the airport and in Kathmandu upon arrival. Having travelled as much of this world as I can afford my mind is fairly open to all things and I try not to pre-judge anything at all. We left Heathrow on **28/03/2008** for Doha where we changed flights to Kathamandu. The first 24hrs of the trip was all about travelling and the time zone changes. We all met in the airport at Kathamandu on **29/03/2008** at around 16:45.

All members of the team (Me, Dave, Carol, Jenny, Penny, John, Tony, Helen, Tony and Jackie, Fred, Colin, Wilf, Chris and Richard, the trek leader) met and got along famously from the off. Not really worth mentioning but throughout the whole experience only two people segregated themselves from the group for reasons best known to them. That's enough of that. Kathmandu even at that time of day was really hot, I helped the Sherpas put the luggage onto the roof of our transport (they were so small, but very strong). We then set off to the Hotel Vaishali, Kathmandu's 4 star hotel (trust me this was 4 stars too many!). The people stared at us in wonder as we did in return, what an eclectic mix of organised chaos at every corner. It seemed like chaos on the move, especially the traffic, street vendors, old oil barrels lit up and cooking cashew and roasted nuts to sell. Buildings defied gravity, half finished or leaning badly but every space was utilised. Car and motorbike horns incessantly being sounded, so looking forward to getting away from all the noise (I love solitude). The hotel was really nice (in a non judgemental way) and was a million miles away from how the locals lived in terms of facilities and class. The electricity worked sometimes and the swimming pool was covered in algae but the people from the off were fantastic and eager to please.

After a little sabbatical we all met in the early evening and proceeded to the Jesse James bar for a group meal. I ordered the combo mix with cold vegetables, surprisingly it tasted good. The lights were low so maybe it was best not seen (only kidding), managed to call my beautiful wife from the resident internet café (very cheap). On the walk back to the hotel the beggars and hashish sellers were everywhere and would not take no for an answer (solitude looms!!). I bought some bottles of water (as advised) because the tap water was a funny colour and not usable. Remember I said earlier not to judge things as we enjoy them and anyway it helps the local economy somewhat if you subscribe to it. For now though it was off to bed to listen to the incessant horns being blasted throughout the night (do they not sleep?).

One hopes that you will find my diary of events interesting. The aim is to try and capture the moment as I saw it. Rather than make up narrative my hope is that you will gain a picture from my words. Often I was just totally amazed and awestruck at all that I saw and shared throughout the whole trip. It proved to me what a wonderful world we actually share and take part in. I feel lucky that I was able to afford such a trip; my further hope is that I get to see as much of this world as I can. God willing I will be in a fit enough state to enjoy it, I just love the world and all it offers.

KATHMANDU 30/03/2008

Today, with the aid of our leader (Richard) we explored a little bit of Kathmandu. We visited the Monkey Temple high on a mountain side, a mixed religion temple (it can work!!). I said prayers for all family and friends both past and present. We were also accompanied by our 3 main Sherpas, Nawang (Sherpa), Perba (Tamang) and Bir (Tamang).

In the afternoon we were let loose to explore Kathmandu where we found you can buy a replica of absolutely any top named climbing brand and became involved in the noble art of bartering. One can literally order, be measured up and collect the same day. In fact the copies are as good as the named brand, if not better at times. Kathmandu itself is very messy and could be cleaner, however I am not the judge. People were extremely friendly for all manner of reasons and not just the money you brought to spend.

Our collective group continue to bond, a mix of thinkers, jokers and orators from the age of 20 to retired. Bed early tonight for an early flight to Lukla, we must go to the airport around 04:30 and fly at 06:30.

KATHMANDU AIRPORT TO LUKLA 31/03/2008

You have to be at the airport to believe it, it really needs to be seen through your own eyes. Upon arrival we were briefed to say no to every question asked, literally throw your bags and I do mean throw your bags at the scanner. I'm not even sure that it was on, a little airport official was running around placing stickers on your bags to prove scanning had been completed.

The plane was a 16 seater and the flight was approximately 40 minutes long. The scenery from above was truly a sight to behold. Then comes the landing, we none of us had ever been to Lukla before except the Trek Leader. We started diving and our eyes strained to see a runway, then when it did appear we could not believe how small it actually was. The landing strip is in a valley sided by two mountains, and is approximately 400metres in length. You land, brake hard, turn towards the airport lounge area (very small) and get out on one side of the plane whilst people returning to Kathmandu get in on the other side. They do not turn the engine off because the air temperature is so low they may not get it started again. They get the people in and go off down the runway which is actually downhill. The plane drops into the valley then rises (thankfully) having seemed like it was going off the edge of the world. We went into the airport, picked up our bags and went straight out the other side into Lukla where we settled in a Café and met our Sherpa carrying team. We were at a starting height of 2652m.

From Lukla we picked up our daysacks and started walking towards our first night in a place called Phakding. The journey took 3hrs and was kept purposefully slow to assist acclimatisation. The route followed the Dudhkoshi river which is called the milky river for the right (colour) reason. There were lots of people on the trail as well as lots of yaks, you have to keep to the inside of a yak in case they are disturbed when they will push you out of the way. We crossed a number of cable and wooden bridges and the scenery was too stunning for any words invented. Surrounded by ice covered peaks (Kumala).

We arrived at our bunkhouse in Phakding, called Sunrise Lodge. There were a few hours of free time which I used to walk into the village. Children would stare innocently, some with and some without footwear. Tourism makes this a rich area with people of all nationalities around, all very friendly. Some Japanese pensioners were actually camping in the field next to us, the next morning they were all exercising ahead of breakfast, truly a sight to be seen.

PHAKDING TO MONJO 01/04/2008
Phakding to Monjo a 3hr walk to Lailash Lodge.

A small altitude rise again to assist acclimatisation. The people of Nepal live very spartan lives, nothing however is too much trouble. To observe young people working extremely hard would both amaze and appal people. We are talking young children as well as teenagers, perhaps we ought to send some of our young to live this life and realise just how fortunate they are.

In Monjo we visited the local school built from funds donated by the Sir Edmund Hillary trust and a German trust.

The rank structure in Nepal is very strictly adhered to, from poor to porter and Sherpa. Each has a defined role, porters, carrying 70kg loads on a strap on their foreheads, is an amazing sight, H&S eat your heart out. These boys deserve everything, not forgetting some are wearing open toed sandals to walk in.

The only difficulty with this journey is in finding the words to explain all that you see, simply if you want to know what I mean you have to visit yourself. Some will see it as the best, I see it as equal in its own right. I'm going to enjoy losing all track of time.

171

MONJO TO NAMCHE 02/04/2008

Monjo to Namche (4hrs, 11,200ft) Khumbu Lodge, on the trail today at 9,700m we saw Everest for the first time in the distance - WOW.

A long slow climb today and now conscious of more effort in breathing, speed is not the order of the day. We crossed the longest cable bridge of the journey and learned that all bridges had recently been replaced due to landslides in the previous two years. The lodge today was in the most spectacular place, almost at the highest point in the valley with a commanding view of all of Namche itself, you truly felt regal.

Me and David roomed together, initially we had the worst room but due to my charm and cheek we were upgraded to one of the best rooms. Jealousy loomed! We were to spend two days here to increase our acclimatisation. I could explain all that I saw, photos could show you, but to appreciate what I saw you would do better to look through your own eyes. I seek not to detract from a detailed explanation, just to say that to experience it for yourself would clearly explain more than the words that I know. As for people who will never go you must close your eyes and dream.

The afternoon was free for us to explore Namche itself, every nook and cranny is utilised with children washing clothes in the stream (freezing). People were looking at us in expectant hope that we would buy something. The walk up and down most certainly tests your lungs. The view across Khumbu is truly breathtaking. Namche has its very own bakery, and when you think that they had to carry all the parts up to this location is no mean feat. The cakes were divine. Mass building was going on everywhere you looked, no doubt to allow even more tourists to visit. One hopes that they have it under control and at some stage they will say this is enough. I don't wish to be selfish to those who are yet to see this beautiful place but seek to say enough is enough without cutting into natural beauty.

03/04/2009 Second day in Namche, today a 5.5hr trip has been planned to assist acclimatisation and see Mount Everest, albeit from a distance. We visited the villages of Khumjung and Khunde, taking in the school built with funding from the Sir Edmund Hillary foundation. Local women were digging and planting potatoes in a field, each carrying babies strapped to their backs. There were yaks pulling along a plough in another field, extraordinarily in reality with the situation, no modern ploughs or machinery here. We viewed a landing strip built for Everest Base Camp (EBC), however it was so badly built that the only planes to try and land actually crashed. Hence the landing strip was closed before it was opened, sadly modern trends and demand may supply the funds to make it viable for those that do not wish to trek the whole way. Mountains we viewed from our vista point, looking left to right: Khumbila, Taboche, Nuptse ridge, Everest, Lhotse, Lhotse Shar, Peak 38, Amadablam (my favourite mountain), Kusumkhangri and Tramcerku.

Back into Namche, we then all met at the bakery to enjoy fresh cakes before our departure the next day. I bought a Mammut jacket 1000r = £8, probably a fake but a very good copy. Jokes about altitude sickness are now wearing thin!!

NAMCHE TO TENGBOCHE 04/04/2008
Namche to Tengboche 6hrs (Oxygen 86 – Pulse 61). Thyangboche Guest House, 11,200ft start, down to 10,600m (river crossing) and then 12,400ft finish.

The day was quite tough. A very steep descent followed by an even harder ascent, the porters who carry everything along this supply/tourist route must be highly commended as they are always smiling at you. To cross the river we travelled across a replacement bridge as the previous one (which you can still see) had collapsed in a landslide.

Arriving at Tengboche 1330 we settled quickly into our lodge then came out and visited the local monastery. As a mark of respect we had to take off our footwear, it was very cold. Then rather bizarrely it started snowing, which we were told is uncommon for this time of year. It soon became a picture postcard scenario. Dave was not feeling too well today. Tengboche itself was the original basecamp for Sir Edmund Hillary prior to his epic climb.

The evening ended in a sing song with songs written by two of our colleagues from Ireland. It was a fantastic end to the day.

05/04/2008 Tengboche to Pangboche 2.15hrs 12500ft. Oxygen 87 – Pulse 55 Shreedewa Lodge

We set off on a snow laden track, lots of activity on the route today with trekkers, yaks and porters etc. The higher we get the higher the prices become, a different country but the rules are constant throughout this world. I purchased chocolate over one year past its sell by date (tasted nice). Telephone prices:

- Kathmandu 25R Per min
- Namche 80R Per min
- Pengboche 200R Per min

The lodge had a proper sit down toilet as opposed to squat, we had arrived in heaven!

After lunch we visited a Gompa, local church to you and me. We also looked at a prayer location where Nuns come and pray in isolation from one month to a year and more.

PANGBOCHE   TO   DINGBOCHE   06/04/2008
Pangboche to Dingboche 3.15hrs 13800ft, staying here for 2 days acclimatisation.

It snowed all day today, extra layers of clothing on to keep the cold at bay. Today also we have been hit by sickness in the camp, with three people suffering, taking tablets and going straight to bed. For the first (noticeable) time we all became conscious of planting our feet and concentrating without too much looking around whilst on the move. If you did look around whilst moving, physically your body demanded some short breaths to regain its synchronisation.

A group of us went walkabout in the afternoon and climbed to 14,200ft and back again. We came off trail though and the guide almost lost his bearings. I have to confess to missing my wife, having waited so long to find happiness it will be a long time before I leave her again.

07/04/2008 Dingboche Oxygen 83 – Pulse 82 (beginning to work now)

Today we climbed a peak aptly named "Little Bugger", it took us to a height of 16,050ft and back to 13,800ft. The sun shone brightly this day and everywhere I looked the main mountain to stand out was Amadablam. We observed eagles using the air currents to effortlessly float in the sky.

Sometimes I have dreams of places that I have never been to. This morning as I stood outside the lodge it suddenly flashed back. I had seen this place before, so maybe my visit was meant to be. It was so cold this morning that we had ice on the inside of our room windows. Inching ever closer to the reason why we all came Everest Base Camp.

On the way down from Little Bugger three of us, including the trek leader, decided to have a race, running down to the lodge. We enjoyed a hot shower and I fell asleep instantly and slept like a log that night. I also had a slight headache which was relieved by two tablets.

DINGBOCHE TO LOBUCHE 08/04/2008
Dingboche to Lobuche 5.5hrs 16,000ft.

The highlight of today's long and slow climb was a visit (on the way) to the Sherpas and climbers cemetery. Point to note is that not all stones raised in the memory of people claimed and killed by the mountain have the actual bodies in place. Some are still on the mountain waiting to become exposed, or not. The most famous person in the cemetery at the time of my visit was a Sherpa named Babu Tshering. For the following reasons:

- He reached the summit of Everest 10 times
- He completed the fastest ascent (at that time) 16hrs 56mins
- He spent 21hrs on the summit
- He sadly died on his 11th attempt after falling in a crevice

We are now in sight of the border between Nepal and Tibet.

The simplicity of life in Nepal is just that, for me I will live it their way until I leave. The beauty of all that I have seen will remain in my mind until I leave this planet. It truly is an experience never to be forgotten, all should visit even if only to Lukla.

That afternoon we had a short walk to look at the Lobuche glaciers, very dangerous. It's bed early tonight as tomorrow we leave at 04:00. When I get back to the UK I need to put all my books down and allow all of this to sink in. I still think that it can be split into 3 thirds. One third is my story, the 2nd third is my photos and the last third you need to come and see for yourself.

LOBUCHE TO GORAP SHEK 09/04/2008
Lobuche to Gorap Shek 3hrs 16800ft. Buddha Lodge

At 04:00 with our head torches on we set out to climb to Gorap Shek, very cold this morning. The climb was led by Nawang our head Sherpa, this route is very dangerous and has claimed lives over the years. Some lives claimed have never been found.

After breakfast at the lodge we set out to climb a practice peak for all Everest Basecamp climbers called Kalapattar. A round trip of 5hrs, the effort of climbing has now become arduous, even at this altitude. The top of Kalapattar is 18,129ft. The views from it are amazing, Everest stand out like a sore thumb, clearly showing the Khumbu ice fields from base camp that all have to navigate at the start of ascent. Most climbers that lose their lives do so navigating the ice fields and to base camp 1.

All bar one of our group made it to the top, one lady sadly stopped 250ft from the top, still a massive achievement.

GORAP SHEK TO EVEREST BASE CAMP (EBC) 10/04/2008

Gorap Shek to EBC 3hrs 17,300ft and Gorap Shek to Lobuche 2.15hrs

Today we climbed to EBC, the camp was already full of tents housing climbers awaiting a suitable temperature to climb Everest. The Khumbu ice fields route is cut each year dependant upon amount of ice and temperature. This area is very dangerous, EBC was very busy and we were allowed only so far into it. Well we all made it, some though are suffering badly, however they will pick up now we are descending. My legs are a little tired but I'm too elated to care.

The mood within the group has changed now as we make our descent and get back slowly to our normal lives. Although the journey is not yet at an end it has more than fulfilled a dream. The scenery that I have seen is almost unexplainable in beauty and grandeur. I thank my wife for allowing me to do this, however my energies will now go into making our lives and dreams together come true.

The people of Nepal are a very hardy race, just like us they are driven by change, some of it you like and some of it you do not. I have witnessed feats of strength and endurance that would make the strongest man or woman seem weak. They have made my journey through their country that much better. A big thanks to all, which also sounds inadequate.

LOBUCHE TO TENGBOCHE 11/04/2008

Lobuche to Tengboche 7hrs loss of height = 3,300ft

Although a long day it was a most enjoyable one. Taking in Pheriche, and changing route at Dughla and Tsuroog following Lobuche Khala. The sights and sounds are amazing, how do the porters do it, women as well. They carry 70kg loads with a small strap on each forehead (Health & Safety). Equally they always get to camp before we do and all we carry are day sacks. Our sick have now recovered considerably, again three of us decided to race, seemed a good idea at the time but very tiring I can assure you.

Tomorrow back in Nmache and fresh cakes, all are excited plus shopping for two days. The trip itself has asked questions of us all, no matter whether physical or mental they all had to be answered and overcome. One group we met along the way started with 15 people and they were down to the last surviving two. All the rest had been taken off the trek, so as you can see it claims anyone it wants, all the rest of their team were transported back down the mountain.

TENGBOCHE TO NAMCHE 12/13/08/2008
Tengboche to Namche 4.5hrs

Throughout the route back so far everyone has commented upon just how high we had climbed, my does the return route look different.

Namche = Shower and Cake Shop

All are pretty tired today, how can I possibly explain this trip to anyone that asks, maybe I should just say 'go see for yourself'. If you truly have a love of the great outdoors this trip will give you everything. It will evoke emotions that you have never felt and the scenery is absolutely stunning.

That evening I decided to try the Yak steak and almost straight away became ill, straight out bed, gallons of water feeling pretty sorry for myself the whole 24hrs.

179

NAMCHE TO LUKLA 14/04/2008
Namche to Lukla 8hrs

A long day, we stopped for dinner in Phakding, then onward to Lukla. Whilst in Phakding we met many groups just starting on the way up, whilst not experts we knew how much effort they must expend just to get to EBC. We certainly felt good because our journey was over, they had just begun.

In Lukla we had a shower and a celebratory meal: Tomato soup, chicken, boiled rice, vegetables, chips, salad and cake.

It was a lovely end to our trip. We were then invited to leave behind any equipment we wanted to for the Sherpas. They in turn shared the equipment given in a very strict pecking order, we also gave them money.

LUKLA TO KATHMANDU 15/04/2008
Lukla to Kathmandu Hotel Vaishali

The airport experience just has to be seen and experienced to be believed. It is organised chaos that somehow seems to work and is run by the Nepalese army. The queue was large and we had to hold our own to get on one of the first planes to Kathmandu.

Kathmandu is almost 30 degrees, in stark contrast to the cold weather we left behind, straight into car and bike horns and the incessant begging from all quarters, which I have not missed. Back to the hotel for a day of shopping; Mammut jacket, t-shirts printed, postcards, just some of the things purchased today.

This evening we had a group meal, all attended except two who have isolated themselves through sheer ignorance, they were not missed. We had a great meal at the New Orleans restaurant, fantastic atmosphere.

KATHMANDU 16/04/2008
Kathmandu Hotel Vaishali

Our final day in Kathmandu before flying home the next day, it was very hot again today, sadly I don't enjoy the heat. I spent most of the day shopping for mountain running shoes to no avail. I did get my hair cut, very professional although they tried to sell me hundreds of extras.

That afternoon we all met in the hotel for flight details, myself and Dave were told we had no flight. Fortunately I spotted the error and we obtained tickets to leave the next day.

We visited a temple and in the evening we had a themed group meal, all sat on a cushion on the floor. Me not being supple struggled with this, wild boar was the main meat and was very nice. Entertained by dancers, we bought and delivered a special thank-you card for our tour leader Richard.

We walked back to the hotel and said our good byes to those not travelling the next day. All members had truly made this a wonderful experience.

THANKS TO NEPAL AND ALL ITS MEMORIES

KATHMANDU TO DOHA 17/04/2008
Kathmandu to Doha & Doha to London Heathrow

Most of what I have written followed a compilation of each day's events I recorded in a diary. Nepal, what small part I have seen is a wonderful place, like most countries the towns are eclectic and cater for all tastes. Then the amazing countryside, its beauty is truly magnificent and stunning. I hope that as many people as possible get to see this part of the world along with many other countries which are equally as stunning. As in each country we care to talk about its population are trying to live their lives as best they can. Some better than others, no matter the country we are equal in its struggle.

I have a piece of rock picked up from EBC on the base of my PC at home. No doubt when I leave this earth it will probably be thrown out as just any old stone. If it does then where it chooses to lie will form a part of history from another part of this planet.

**Standing on Kalapathar 18,129ft 09/04/2008,
EVEREST directly above my head**

Chapter IX

Alcohol and Alcoholism

I sincerely hope as you travel through this chapter that I do it justice, my hope is that it is not contradictory and that having read it, **it might, just might** give you and others the strength you require to actually do something about it. I must also stress that these views and thoughts are my own and are in no way to be misconstrued as the way everyone should do it. It is quite simply my way and it more than fits my world.

I took my last drink on 11 October 2004

It is supposed that the first question is why did I stop drinking or indeed want to? It was **NOT, repeat NOT,** because I thought I was an **alcoholic**, although those that read this (and are recovering alcoholics) will probably say "is he sure?" To be true to my thought processes though it has to be said that I totally enjoyed drinking over the 25 plus years that I did it. A lot of fun was had by myself and others, no harm to anyone but myself (in the drinking group not family or partners). Little did I realise the **addictive power** of it or the grip it would get on my life or the damage it would do within a relationship. It only became an issue when I no longer enjoyed doing it, every week the same repetition, drink, talk shit, more drink, more shit (some of the talk was good though). It was at this stage and probably before if I am honest that I realised that I was not totally in control of the decision to drink or not (especially NOT!). Equally it matters little now what I thought or why, what does matter is that I stick to my resolve of never drinking alcohol again. I don't question why I used to drink. Equally I don't question why I no longer drink. Remember **KEEP IT SIMPLE**. First the pattern of my drinking throughout 25 years:

- I drank every single day, in the week small to large amounts but at the weekend massive amounts. Total alcoholic oblivion was guaranteed
- My tolerance level for what it's worth was extremely high, always drinking to capacity and sometimes (often) beyond, like it was some achievement to drink the most (how stupid that sounds now)
- I could not stop for some reason, still unknown, to this day
- I did not know the difference between one and 20 drinks
- Party invites were never refused, positively encouraged with or without a good reason
- Travelling to different countries to sample the delights of alcohol, which included invitations from strangers (and I always turned up)
- 13 years in the British Army (notorious for hard drinking)
- Scars on my body which include being glassed whilst drinking, all it proves is that I got away with it and was equally stupid
- Dutch courage gained from drinking and the stupid things your sizzled brain allows you to do just for a laugh. Too many to mention
- Fights (not proud of this one)
- Hiding the drink around the house and buying spare (full) bottles so my partner could not see how much I was drinking

- Wine, beer, spirits, anything that would fit in a glass

I must stress at this point that unlike others I did not drink to fit in or indeed drink because I felt left out. I was and am a confident person in my own right; fully aware of my capabilities at all levels.

The decision to actually stop was at least, from memory, two to three years in the making. Each weekend (prior to actually stopping) I would tell myself to drink hard, as from Monday it would all be over. But the Mondays kept coming and going. Over the years people had commented on my drinking, we are talking vast amounts here. Don't get me wrong I knew I had to work on a Monday and in the week, this was never affected. But, and there is always a damned but, towards the end I was edging closer to oblivion on a Sunday more than ever. Instead of drinking from 12:00 to 16:00 it was ever extending until 22:30 in the evening and sometimes later. Only once in my life did I miss a Monday start because I finished drinking at 02:00 and still woke up for work at 04:30 but decided I was not fit to drive to London that day, boy did I feel like shit and probably looked it too. This was surely a big warning sign. Again it really does not matter how much I could drink but I kept on doing it. I have never been sick or urinated on anyone. A couple of times I urinated in the wardrobe not knowing where I was. I had stitches without anaesthetic because I was so drunk on one occasion, how I got away with the accident I will never know. Two of us actually climbed a brickyard chimney stack to hoist a flag for a photograph the next day. The brickyard had been derelict for years; I fell off the ladder on the side of the chimney coming down and going straight through the roof of the surrounding building. This was at 04:30 in the morning as drunk as one can be and encouraged by others. Fights galore, nothing proud in that statement either, once sober the pain set in I can assure you. It was nullified initially because of the drink. The pattern of hiding it was not really an issue (or was it?), all bills were paid.

One thing I am absolutely proud of is that I never drank and drove. However I did drive the next day, so that might not actually be a completely true statement.

I was asked one day on a Health & Safety training course to drink and be breathalysed the next day as a test for the examiner. I drank on this occasion four bottles of Becks, two glasses of white wine, four pints of Stella Artois and three brandies. I stopped drinking at midnight and was tested at 10:00 the next morning and registered a nil reading. I'm not bragging you understand, if you like trying to justify driving the next day, as I did not always drink that much in the week. It was getting close towards the end though.

My drinking, for what it was, started when I joined the Army at 19 and a half years of age. No one put a drink into my hand I might add but I was happy to take it. The hit from alcohol was amazing; the first pint really went through my body like a blood rush, even at the end of my drinking. The problem was that right from day one I carried on drinking until I was full or had to sleep. The tolerance and quantity drunk increased as the years went on. I was an absolute swine at drinking spirits once full from beer, three scars on my body prove it.

Alcohol though was never a part of my growing up years, Mum never drank ever and Dad stopped drinking when I was 7 years old through **willpower** alone (Dad was certainly strong in mind). Like other people I never started drinking at an early age as my Mum would have killed me and fair play to her for it. I clearly remember the estate I lived on, every Sunday you would see the menfolk wobbling home after a Sunday session at the pub. Some even had to be assisted, often by their wives. I mentioned earlier that I did not stop because I thought I was an alcoholic but the strength of this drug takes hold of you and is no different any other drug. Once it takes hold it's hard and often difficult to stop. People have sadly lost their lives because of it and others struggle. Those in society who can take it or leave it have my utmost admiration and total respect. For me it really is the end of drinking, it is beyond my own personal control to drink one or two and leave it. Both Mum and Dad commented over the years but they never thought I was or could be an alcoholic. Dad simply said you can stop if you want to; my Dad did through willpower alone for the last 39 years of his life. Mum saw me totally sober for 18 months before she died and was as proud of me as Dad was. I remember sitting with Dad one evening, quietly watching TV. He turned to me and said "you know Dean that you can never drink again", "yes Dad" I replied. That was it with Dad no more needed to be said, if I was to drink again Dad would have been unforgiving and simply said "it's because you're weak". It is my wish that I honour those words until the day that I myself die. That we will not know until I do, however I will give it my best shot.

My last drink in bold earlier in this chapter was 11/10/2004, the next day I was finally going to do something about it. On the 12/10/2004 I approached the Samaritans and asked for help. They duly gave me the number of Alcoholics Anonymous, whom I called and was invited to a meeting of other people suffering from the same addiction. God was I nervous, having to join people and admit you had an issue filled me with fear. To make it worse when I walked in I met an old friend I used to drink with, now he knew as well. Well let me tell you, no finer people could you wish to meet, worth pointing out that not one of them has ever called me or anyone an alcoholic. The support you can get would amaze you, these are the best of people, all from varying backgrounds (including the very rich if you're interested).

The first days and weeks flew by; please allow me to make a point which is totally my very own OPINION (Chapter VIII, No 10). My parents gave me a thoroughly wonderful upbringing and I will die forever preaching all that they taught me to whoever will listen. Like my father, once I enter a process I am 100% committed to it, once I had controlled my mind again, just like I was taught to as a child. Hopefully now this will carry me through without drink for the rest of my life.

It is not my wish to state how the AA is run or formed and what syllabus it follows. The script is simple and varied to suit each person's individual needs. The only thing it asks in return is total application, this simple point once followed will allow you to put drink down and never pick it up again. You only have to stop drinking for one day at a time.

So how did I stop drinking and stay stopped for over 8 years now, once again what I am about to write works for me only. Some points however may be practiced by others but probably not all.

- **I told both Mum and Dad that I would never drink again, to which they replied we believe**

you. I will endeavour to never let them or myself down.

- My application to stopping drinking was totally firm from day one (12/10/2004)

- I love being able to tell people I no longer drink, the reactions are sometimes amazing. Apparently I do not look like a person who doesn't drink or has a problem with it (now just what does that mean? Never realised it had its own identification)

- Total elimination of any thoughts or reasons why I used to drink. All the reasons why I took a drink will be around until the day that I die, the only thing required of me is never to pick up a drink again

- Total support from my wife (who has never seen me drink) and from my two brothers (who were big drinking buddies) and all my close friends (excluding those drinking buddies who no longer talk to or see me)

- Rarely these days do I just go to a pub; still I attend functions and parties as invited. Not to test myself you understand. It is imperative at times that I can cope with this addiction but not to test it.

- Such is my strength of mind I pass days, weeks and months without ever thinking of drinking, as I used to. And I do mean never thinking about it.

- Being truthful and not hiding the fact that I had an issue, this is not for everyone but it works for me.

- Leading a very full and active life as I did when I was at my peak of power. (Still got some left although it seems to be selective these days as to when it appears!)

- I attend **AA** meetings as I choose; initially I used to go at least 3 or 4 times a week. Now though I go only once a week and often I don't go for a few weeks or months, please note that this attendance requirement would be questioned by the AA's policy and beliefs. It is my own very personal journey and it is not the way we all do it. You can go to as many as you wish, seven days a week twice a day if necessary.
- Use of **<u>Trigger Points</u>** especially in the early days to instantly ward off any reasons why I should have a drink. Any of the above were instant, in particular my thoughts of Mum and Dad and what I had said to them which I personally hold very dear.

So in everything that we do in our lives all one has to do is subscribe to it no matter what it is. I will list just a few things we do, sometimes not giving it a thought as to why. However it all boils down to the same thing we subscribed to it:

- Marriage, relationships etc.
- Gym membership
- School, college, and university
- Parenthood
- Work

The list above is not exhaustive but it should make it clear in your mind the things we do naturally without thought or regard as to why. Simply put, all I now have to do for the rest of my days is subscribe to not drinking. Something I do not take lightly, as I said before though, days, weeks and months pass by and I never, repeat never, even think about alcohol. All my little schemes and plans to obtain a drink each and every day have been eradicated by me in my own mind. And yes cats are still going to cross the road safely without me having to have a drink to celebrate for the cat!

Sadly I have met many people who want to control their drinking but have failed to do so and carry on or start again shortly after. No one can be forced; it is all about knowing yourself as an individual. For myself I have a compulsive nature, that's why I do not know the difference between one and 20 drinks. Each time I drank I wanted the hit, sometimes it came quickly and other times slowly. It all pales into insignificance now though as my journey through life takes on a new meaning. **As long as I keep believing in myself, nothing will alter it but me**. One question I asked myself relatively early into my sobriety was "can you still have as much fun without the drink?" I am duty bound to say yes of course you can. After all having fun is as much about a feeling of timing drunk or sober. Also when the night ends you know where you are, who you are and more importantly where it is that you are going.

So what can or does being full of beer do to a person whether male or female:

- Beauty enhancer (male and female alike)
- Bravery, not seeing the true potential of danger in the circumstance
- Wet yourself or even worse sh*t yourself (often in bed)
- Dance like you think you can!
- Lights up at the end of the night (who's left)
- Fight because now you have become the best fighter in the world
- No feeling of pain, until you sober up that is!

- Be sick, wherever it spouts or which end it comes from!
- SEX with a stranger, usually wishing the next day that you had not!

Anyway let's get back on track, if you truly want to stop drinking and are having difficulty doing so as long as you are capable of subscribing you will find support. Groups of people such as the AA and other renowned organisations will greatly assist you; your input is to keep going back to the meetings. You will also meet a variety of people, some you will like and others tolerate. It's no different to anywhere in life you choose to tread, it will hurt initially but with a lot of application you can do it. I remind you of a saying from my Dad again "**Keep it simple**". Because we forever complicate our lives or allow them to be blighted by this world, we sometimes fail. Those strong enough to pick themselves up will get through it. The AA suggests that you gain a sponsor who will assist you through the programme. I myself have never sought a sponsor nor do I wish to, my sponsors from day one were myself, my parents, my wife, my family, my friends and the AA room members. The importance of sponsors is not to be undervalued; it is just my own personal choosing not to have one. Having no desire to talk about drinking I see no point but totally understand that it is of great help to others. It is my belief that all sayings, traditions and steps as depicted in the AA are what we practice throughout life anyway. Some better than others and some not at all. Look forwards and not backwards. Reminding ourselves of these is the key to success, once it becomes second nature you should be well on the way to recovery.

The path through life I have now chosen without alcohol (and many other things) is truly wonderful. It would be easy to say I wished that I had stopped earlier, but as Mum would say "everything has its timing and happens for a purpose".

Some Notable/Noble ABSTAINERS from alcohol both past and present:

- Field Marshall Montgomery (2nd World War Leader)
- Sir Anthony Hopkins (Actor)
- Robbie Williams (Singer)
- Me (Dean Horobin-Wright) author of this book
- Lord Wolseley (Soldier)
- Sir John Ross (Sailor)
- John Wesley (preacher)
- Dr Gutherie (Author of "The City: Its Sins and Its Sorrows")
- John Bright (Quaker)
- Robin Williams (Actor)
- John Hurt (Actor)

Behind the mist of the craving for ALCOHOL what DAMAGE do we as human beings ACTUALLY do to ourselves, our partners, our families and society?

- First, and most important of all, it's an **ADDICTION** that tells us we don't have a problem! **This statement is definitively TRUE**
- Destroys liver and brain sense (conversation)
- Ruins working life
- Destroys relationships
- **The people I feel sorry for the most are the innocent children, especially as they have no influence on what the parent or parents do. When they are old enough to make choices the**

damage has been done and it takes strong children not to follow suit. They are often dragged from pillar to post, from pub to pub until the parents are satisfied with their own intake. Who I might ask gets up in the night in the event of an emergency? They witness a lot more than the parents give them credit for (trust me). It may come back later in life and bite the parents on the bum. I have made this piece in BOLD so that if any parent with an issue with alcohol reads this they will be overcome with some kind of shame or guilt. Hopefully it will also give them the strength to sort it out, for themselves first and family second.

- Commit acts of crime no matter how petty, stealing money or even the drink itself
- Ruin (in time) natural body functions
- Sleeping rough and often dirty (dishevelled)
- Alienate ourselves from living as we know and understand it
- Social outcasts
- Results in DEATH

"NEVER LET AN EXCUSE BE THE REASON WHY YOU DON'T DO IT"

I feel it fair to point out that the main reason I will (hopefully) never drink again is because I told my Mum and Dad that I would not. This along with my all or nothing attitude will last me until the day that I die.

Chapter X

A Miscellany of Thoughts and/or Opinions!

The following represents my thoughts as I journey through life, the day, driving along to work (where I think most) etc. Nothing is set in stone and upon reflection I could or even should change some points. I am willing to bet that for some of you a large portion of what you will read in this chapter has already been discussed in your own lives. It does not seek to tell or indeed ask that you agree. These are merely my thoughts and reflections. In fact where does one draw an end to this chapter, stay positive, reflect often, dwell upon little and enjoy this life.

Note the dictionary definition of the word OPINION! :

1.   **Life:** as we all know is all about ups and downs. If however you can upon reflection see that the ups outweigh the downs then trust me you are doing ok. Obviously a life with no downs is preferable but unfortunately it's a fact of life. Equally if we put as much effort into being happy as we do in being sad then surely it would be a much better world.

2.   **Excuse:** One of the worst words in the dictionary (of which there are many) is the word excuse. I mentioned it at the beginning of this book, **"never let an excuse be the reason why you don't do it".** To our Dad life was seen in simple terms, he lived by these sayings his whole life. If we think about it though, he is right. How often have you come up with

an excuse not to do something for any number of reasons? God knows I myself have used them, but when I have applied this strictly in my life they have been the much happier times. So come on cut out the excuses and make positive happier changes to your life. Remember this, once the day, time or event has passed you can never go back and change it.

3. **Everything we say or read is a representation/interpretation of the truth**. So why do I say that? All history has an interpretation as written by the biographer or auto-biographer. The stories we tell as human beings to each other are often added to for effect. This book is my version of events which could be questioned by those that know me. It's not to say that anything is a lie, just often not the correct version of events in other people's opinions.

4. **Everything that is allegedly famous has been created by rich, titled or regal people**. Today we pour millions in all over this world visiting monuments and buildings which the original owners can no longer afford to run. When they could afford them we were not allowed into them at all. Now they ask us to pay and visit the bits they allow us to see, absolutely ludicrous, they call it **THE NATIONAL TRUST**. I live for the day when this ends, don't get me wrong I am all for maintaining historical monuments. But not when in my own interpretation it means they can live in splendour funded by us. Now please forgive me in that I know that if you can afford it you can have anything built for you. The problem is in my mind is that many can no longer afford it so in order to maintain the lavish lifestyle they allow the poor serfs (me and you) a little bit of access to a world, ordinarily, most of us would never see or take part in. Back to other references in my

book, that if you could just keep it simple, then you would enjoy your own world. I do visit historic houses by the way (contra indication). **National Trust Member!**

5. **History**: this just happens to be a favourite subject of mine and I read books profusely. I have a select number of people I like to read about from yesteryear, not too interested (yet) in anything this modern world gives us. Others will have to make head or tail of what or who we are and exactly what we have given them. I am fascinated by times gone by, as they seemed much slower. Today is a little too fast for my liking. Having read lots of books it seems to me that in fact we are no better off today than they were then. All we do is move things to the next level, having picked up a few more less fortunate people on the way. By that I mean that a class system is as prevalent today as it was back in the 17th century. Only the rules have somewhat changed in that they cannot freely murder you today as they did back then, unless of course it is carried out by the government who will in turn appoint a high powered barrister and deny it! We are still ruled by the rich and sometimes they let the average bloke into their world but only if he or she can satisfy a strict criteria. Of course we are always going to have rebels, as they did back then, but in the whole we are still ruled by the rich and titled gentry. The rules we live by today are often modernised from the past, hence why most of the actual policies that we live by were actually written by Enoch Powell (Life of a Roman) back in the 1950/60/70s. To think that politicians actually employ people to redevelop policies of yesteryear. The Sun newspaper tells them how the people feel every day. Back onto history itself, you only have to read the great Samuel Pepys' diaries to realise how corrupt he was

himself. He is most famous for the diaries he left behind, bet you did not know that he actually did not write for the last 30 years of his life. Don't get me wrong he did what we all must do in life, get through it as best we can and give back to society what it asks of us. We must all contribute to the system to keep it going as we know it. But old Samuel bless him was indeed, as corrupt as his peers only he was better at getting away with it, better solely because of his memory retention and documentation of the facts. Coupled with the odd bit of friendship mongering by good cause or bribery. So you see at the beginning of my book I stated that we all had a story to tell but often die without telling it. He told us part of his and in parts it is a very witty read, especially as it reflects how some of us still live our lives today. James Boswell as well is a fascinating read, again the same as Pepys he courted the right people until he broke through. Of course the books I truly like to read are about people who made a difference and they are too numerous to mention. Albert Schweitzer, Darwin, Montgomery, Churchill, Chaplin, Trenchard, Boswell, Dr Johnson, Florence Nightingale, Dr Burney, George Eliot, Enoch Powell, Einstein and Darwin to name but a few, along with many others gave us reasons to look into the world as we know it and to better understand it. I know you are crying out for lots of other names to be mentioned and I have read more, they are simply to whet the appetite that's all.

6.   **Democracy**: is this the fairest system that we have or just the best of all the alternatives? Don't get me wrong I think it's a good system, question is "does democracy really exist?" I won't dwell on it but it seems to me that if democracy relies on a majority decision, this alone creates a lot of unrest. I know differences of opinion will always exist and no matter

how hard we try we will not please everyone. But if out of 100 people 51 vote yes and the ruling is passed then you are left with 49 angry people. Now multiply to 500,001 out of a million people and that leaves 499,999 angry people. Little wonder why we have so much conflict and difference of opinion going on. It is beyond me to offer an alternative other than tolerating any difference of opinion in your own private world. There is so much to enjoy from actually being alive. Let's face it, democracy by definition means different things in different countries of this world and is dependent on whoever is in power.

7. **Disability**: question "are we any further forward in disability recognition today than we were say 40 years ago?" The next points are my opinion only. Whilst a lot of headway has been made in access of all kinds, parking, jobs, etc. it seems to me that the way people deal with disability has changed very little. A lot of disability is still hidden away as people all over this world care for disabled children, partners and family in their own homes. Able bodied people could do more in the voluntary sector (it does not, nor should not, always be paid work) to help people whose lives revolve around the disability. From our very own family experience of living with and looking after our father for 40 years I know it was a constant adaptation to his needs. It seems that no matter how much help is offered it is never enough. A comeback of good old community spirit could help to alleviate the intolerable pressure for carers looking after disabled people. Please do not take anything away from the people that do give up their time (including myself) to assist in care of people. All the people that may read my thoughts, let this be the trigger you are looking for and give of your time unto others. When our father was first disabled

people used to stare at him because he seemed different. 40 years on, just before his death they still stared at him, although we were more tolerant of it. Maybe education could cover it, or good parenting as it used to be. Even today I dislike seeing people who are disabled in any way especially if they are young. It disturbs my heart to think of what lies ahead for them. Although it is appreciated that they can and indeed do live wonderful lives, dependant on the level of their disability.

8.   **Advertising**: this in today's world means "not telling the truth but obtaining great monetary recompense from the customer". If only it would tell the bloody truth, always the hidden meanings are written in such small print you require an opticians magnifying glass to read it. And hey if we make a mistake we all become politicians and manage it out. Would it be possible that they could tell the truth? Are we so naive that we honestly believe you can get something for free with no ulterior motive whatsoever?

9.   **Speeding:** I have no doubt that the word just expressed causes all kinds of feelings and response. I seek in the next words not to give speeding the ok but to pour scorn on the theory that speeding causes accidents. Along with each successive government and local councils fining is a licence to print money. The saddest thing of all is that we have just accepted it as a blight on our lives. Let me start by saying that in today's world technology exists to eliminate speeding at one hit. If the government wanted to they could impose (autocratic) that all cars are fitted with responders (with a selection switch in each car to turn it off if you want to take the chance with speeding/freedom of rights also covered) so that when

you enter a speed restriction area a signal is sent to your engine and it slows down accordingly. Not unlike receiving signals for your satellite navigation system. Sadly though they are now reliant on massive fines as a means of revenue gained so that we can use it to appease the public tax payers. And again we bloody well accept it. At the stroke of one pen we could totally obliterate it, surely there can be no votes against because after all, are we not all law abiding citizens? The ones who wish to speed can turn the selector switch to OFF and carry on speeding and cannot moan once caught. Now as I said at the beginning speed does not cause accidents, what it does though is compound them, a contributory factor. The person or persons who cause accidents are the ones at the steering wheel or the passengers in a car who take away the driver's concentration. If like me you are fed up of seeing incessant signs telling you "in the next 3 miles in the last 2 years we have had 10 accidents". In today's world that does not seem excessive in my opinion, exactly how many of them were caused by the following and are they all tested for at the scene? Drugs of any kind, drink and I know we have a limit but it should be ZERO and nothing else, older folk who are not required to take a review of driving, folk who suddenly become ill or are ill and have suffered an attack, motorcyclists speeding, the list could go on. This paragraph will for sure create controversy from members of the public. Remember though the law does not go far enough to ensure drivers are safe to start the day, nor I suspect can it. How many of us get out of bed straight into the car and drive to work still tired, drinking coffee, clearing a 10inch snow hole, using mobile phones or satnavs, applying make-up with 10 minutes or less to get there. Come on admit it we all do. So now if we use technology to really make it safe and agree upon set speed limits it's the least we can do. But guess what, if any government imposes that, then they must also accept the cost to business because without daily speeding people would not get to work on time.

10. **Opinion:** The absolute worst word ever invented or given a meaning, is the word opinion, it gets worse when you read its dictionary definition **"belief based on grounds short of proof; professional advice (Govt!!). Unduly confident in ones opinions, stubborn"** Please note I added the (Govt!!!) bit myself, only because I am fed up of them all. So what does opinion do for our world, society and common goals. Well it divides countries and people within the country, marriages, partnerships, friends, religion and colour. It then leads to conflict often leading to death of any one of the list in the previous sentence and yes I know that more exist. Opinion is based on the numbers game which is why one half endures the ruling of your particular country and the other half either dies or moves or hopes for change. We often offer opinions which are wrong but if you're anything like any government of today you appoint a top spin doctor to get you out of anything that you're in trouble for. Unless of course you're poor, then you have to accept the consequence. Is it fair, in my opinion (couldn't resist) no it bloody well is not!

11. **Hindsight V Foresight:** Or should it be the other way round? Reason being is that we spend a lot of our time and thought processes looking forward without actually realising it. You can see it in a relationship where you are looking for something that will hold you together during the future. You can see it in the very words you or others use as condolence when something either goes wrong or does not happen. Take

a pause at this stage and rather than be judgemental about it – relax –listen – understand – acknowledge – right let's move on. Everyone has a friend, relative or acquaintance who will always say I told you so; they knew long ago it was wrong. We create so many sayings to hide an issue that we forget how to live with each other as true friends. In all that we know all we need to do is keep it simple. It matters not about hindsight or foresight as long as you the person involved at whatever stage of your lives learns and, more importantly lets go and moves on. **Remember "Life is best understood backwards but must be lived Forwards"**

12. **Life's Journey:** So from birth until the day that we die we travel through life, not a lie but a true fact. We are constantly learning all the way, some things we take in and utilise, as for the rest we discard it because hopefully it does not affect us or cause anyone any trouble (but sometimes it does especially not paying bills). In turn we meet lots of people, some we like and some we don't. The older and possibly wiser we get we tend to make up our minds quickly. This however can have its pitfalls, not really going to explain as we could go on forever. Make up your own mind as to how to fill this picture, suffice to say that if you can keep an open mind then you're a winner. As my good old Dad would have said "the problem with people is that they have forgotten to live life in simple terms". Constantly allowing outside pressures to influence us, in the worst case scenario to the point of death itself. My only advice would be for everyone to read history books, you will soon realise that the world has changed very little. Yet we still allow things to affect the way we live; now I don't suggest for one minute that it's easy. But no matter what we all do, in

order for us to succeed, keep it simple and merely **SUBSCRIBE**. After all I dare say that if you reflect upon your lives hopefully you will comfort yourselves, as I do, with just how much so far I have crammed into it and just how much more god willing I will cram into what's left. So come on forget any troubles and embrace life, it's the only one we have. It does not matter what level you're at, just enjoy it and what it gives. Remember you can change anything but only if you want to. Professors, doctors and psychiatrists write books telling us how to live and enjoy life. Forget them and listen to all that is passed down to you by family and friends and start right now enjoying your journey. And if by telling your story you exaggerate a little, so bloody what. ENJOY IT ALL!

13. **Life in Brief:** Do you not find the way life changes and indeed the way that we ourselves change as we age makes us think differently? For instance:

- When you are young you are totally invincible, this feeling lasts for quite a few years (approximately to your 30s or even 40s). Then all of a sudden you start to feel vulnerable knowing that you cannot react the way that you once could or did.
- What happens to spontaneity of movement, remember when you could just take off and run like the wind? As you get older it suddenly disappears for no reason other than getting old I guess
- You now take longer to warm up, you swing your legs out of bed and then have to pause before moving to avoid falling over
- Rigor mortis sets in well before you die, your joints ache. If like me you have trained

prolifically over the years (still trying) then this I suppose catches you up at some stage

- You could once roll about without thinking, now if you play with the kids you gradually climb down to a lower level because you know it will absolutely hurt if you do not

14. **Sex:** Now then this ought to raise a few eyebrows, why put it into the miscellaneous section? What is it all about? It's something that can preoccupy us through our lives. We frustrate ourselves with how we think it should be and the fact that someone else (usually a friend whose own sex life is not nearly as good as they make out) is having your share of the greatest SEX on planet earth. We read books, magazines, feed off advertisements and often friends, we also watch films where they make love for hours on end. To me the biggest reason we don't have a fulfilling sexual life is because one or both people in the relationship do not communicate effectively about the subject. I know from past relationships that this is the case, personally now I have a wife with whom I can discuss absolutely everything. Not forgetting though that some things are out of bounds with each other. Not to the point of being judgemental thinking that it is better somewhere else because often it is not. Once the sexual frenzy of an initial relationship is over then the hard work begins. This is true, especially in a marriage or long term relationship. Those that choose to have an affair get only one thing different to the relationship they already have and that put simply is SEX with a different person. All the other aspects of a relationship are exactly the same no matter who it is with. If communications along with a lot of other considerations are taken into account then your relationship will work. Like everything else in life you

have to subscribe and make the effort for each other no matter whether you are heterosexual or gay. You do not need me to spell out the myths of a poor or fulfilling sex life. Suffice to say that without continual effort from all involved then it will fail. Just like the diet you keep saying you're going to go on.

15. **Diet**: Dictionary definition again: **way of feeding: prescribed course of food: habitual food: keep to a special diet: course of diet: allowance or character of food provided**: Now let's pause and eat (forgive the pun) into this definition, sometimes I wish that someone would edit dictionaries and change definitions to suit what it is exactly the word means. In this case because of its broad definition I would eradicate it from the dictionary altogether. It should not have a meaning that allows people to get rich off of it (extremely bad English I know). The problem I have with the word is that in my opinion (hate that word) the word diet does not exist. The biggest issue that people have with losing weight is the distinct inability to change their own lifestyle. It even covers that in the definition "habitual food", now how damning is that. Mankind is part of the reason why people pile on weight with all this genetically grown produce and 'ready' meals to cater for the busy person. These types of food are damaging beyond belief, we need to look at how people coped in the 1950s and reduce the ever growing greed of chain supermarkets trying to make us buy products that are knowingly bad for some people. The get-out clause is that for the mainstream these food are ok, but for some, who are fast becoming the majority, the body cannot cope with this influx of crap food. But let's not stop the wonderful profiteers who want to make more money with little appreciation of how miserable some people's lives have become

through the food that they sell. They will simply say that we are offering our customers choice and they should read the extremely small print on the back of each packet. What the world needs is an influx of nutritionists to deal with the ever growing differences between human beings who cannot consume the same foods. That to me is where people fail in not understanding their own body metabolism or indeed have ever been shown how to carry this out. If people were more aware then they could, from an early age, make sensible choices. Now if we all had access to a top grade nutritionist who could safely work with us through the initial years and work out how our bodies deal with foods of all kinds then this could stem the tide of obesity. Sadly we are in a vicious circle of profit v greed v taxes. Now change your lifestyle (or not) and eat well (or not) and remember, all you ever need to be is TRULY HAPPY no matter how big or small you are.

16. **TOLERATE:** Dictionary definition **"Endure, permit; allow to exist, to be practiced, etc. without interference or molestation; forbear to judge harshly; sustain use of without harm"** If I was to keep it simple here I would simply say that we as a whole human race are 100% guilty. How can one word have so many meanings? If we were to individualise each meaning we could write a book on the interpretation alone. I take umbrage at the phrase **"allow to exist"**, now that alone would open a very large can of worms. What or whom exactly can simply be allowed to exist? Everyone has a choice in this world (or do they?), if that were true then simply put it out of your mind and live life to the full. If everyone remembers the three types of person as mentioned in my book at various stages and you have decided that you are indeed an ARTIST. Then everyone has a right

to exist, please note that I am appreciative that some heinous crimes push us to the limit. I do not wish to patronize those that have suffered at the hands of others. As a matter of interest I would vote for the death penalty to return. Only because DNA testing is now almost fool-proof. Perhaps now I am answering for myself and maybe for you all the meanings attributed to one word. If we have an issue with anyone or anything we only have to live in our inner circles in our private lives without the prejudice afforded to those that do not suit your world.

17. **We as human beings have created everything that we suffer from:** Pick from a not too exhaustive list, from the list you will have to think and expand as to the reasons why yourself. I feel sure that one or more will fit life as you know it: genetic food, pollution, wars, medicine of all forms, living standards, inequality or affordability of treatment, lack of choice rather than equality, telling the TRUTH, beliefs and opinions.

18. **Work:** Hopefully throughout our lifetime we will endeavour to be in full time employment. Assuming that's from the age of 16 to 65 this equals 49 years at work. I do know that the retirement age is changing each year to try to manage pension payments, merely used as an analogy. Gone are the days (almost) when you will be employed by the same employer for that length of time. Now I am not an expert on all kinds of employment, but I do know that some are more strenuous than others. This can and often does take its toll on our bodies. How nice it would be to have in the larger industries a therapist, doctor, nutritionist and masseur to name but a few whose role would be to keep the workforce intact. This in itself would allow firms to

keep great minds whose only downfall is to become weak, often by the processes incurred in the job role itself. Yes we have Health & Safety, for them though the job definition requires updating.

Successive governments are continually coming up with ideas to alleviate work pressure measured against lots of other things (growth, jobs etc). That in itself seems unavoidable; it does however distort the truth. We are creating a world full of coffee makers, what we need more than anything is industry. Let's return to apprenticeships where young minds meet and work with older minds.

Work itself is a combination of things, for myself I have been lucky so far in that I have only had two major jobs with a few gap fillers. In my 35 years of working so far I have only been out of work for three months and that was out of choice to allow me to go to college. At college though I was badly let down by the government who had created a scheme where colleges only wanted you to fill certain subjects to allow them access to more funding (that is a FACT). Sorry I digress, back to work being a combination of things; mostly I would hope it was joyous. Equally I understand that we all at times undergo tedious moments at work, constantly thinking that we know better. One assumes that is part of the working arena that we inherit from those before us. What one must do though is go to work to actually work. Go to work because you want to rather than have to. Companies are frustrated with people thinking the latter, become part of doing things because you want to rather than have to.

All the time at work we are constantly heading towards our pensions, and each and every year the government put out statements to the effect that we are not doing enough (unless you're rich and or a banker). This in turn allows each company to say the same and reduce their efforts in the company pension plan whilst inviting you to pay more. Both points are a double whammy, faced with all that just how does one save for a pension. As for myself I have four pensions:

- Army Pension (13 years)
- Private Pension Plan (16+ years) albeit a pitiful one!
- Company Pension Plan 18+ Years (just been reduced because of the deficit in company payments. Now we choose our own plan)
- Government Pension at 67

Now looking at the above you would think it is pretty healthy, allow me to set my thoughts out. The Army pension is currently being reduced which will mean low payments upon maturity. Due to mature at 55, I'm now 51 and the government are putting it up to 60 = thanks very much). The private pension is worth peanuts, they will not allow me to cash it in because of the rules so I'm stuck with it. If it was feasible I would need to increase my payments by 400% to make it worthwhile. The company plan, if I work until I retire, will be 13 years frozen at current level (this used to be a great pension which proved too costly, so the government allowed my company to reduce it within the rules which in turn equals a poorer return) will ensure a pension of 29 years maturity. The government pension will probably not exist by then, it will probably also be means tested against the others which in turn means zero return. So all in all having tried to do what each government asked it looks like I will still be poor. I do hope not!

19. **Equality:** No matter which way this word is painted it does not actually exist, for me it is no better

than any other words driven by a marketing campaign designed to appease. For sure it will pick up a few new members along the way but never an actual total. If you read through all history books whether the truth is known or not, equality has never nor will it ever exist. It's almost as if it has become a SAFE word along with others for leaders to use to address known problems or issues but without the conviction to carry them out. Adaptations of equality have been created but as long as the world is structured the way it is it will never, and possibly cannot, change. We are all involved in a dog eat dog world, struggling to survive just like everyone else. Some tolerate (**see 16**) better than others. But that only creates a small piece of harmony. Successive leaders throughout the years along with monarchies have seen to it that we, the average kids on the block, never climb any higher than we should. Those that do get reined in at some juncture along the route. Not forgetting all the rules in place to make it hard to get through, yes some do get through but in my opinion not enough. No doubt the saying for all the above is "we are simply doing the best that we can" but it's never enough. I do subscribe to a culture where we work and live in harmony and have no desire to pour scorn upon anyone. Equality though as stated at the beginning simply does not exist.

20. **Fair/Fairness:** Unfortunately we are all **inextricably linked** in ensuring that the two preceding words never occur in society. Before you stress yourselves into believing that it does exist please note that I ended my sentence with the word **society**! I feel like I ought to explain that like you I know of people who have made a change to people's lives. Often though this is at the expense (eventually) of a political or beneficial gain. Not necessarily from themselves but

from people with the power to do so. Yes it is also understood that these people should be commended for their actions and rightly so. What I'm talking about is for all members of this world without question. We all believe that if we all do well we can cater for those that cannot, building this never ending circle which we cannot get off. **Circle was chosen for a reason!** Successive leaders and countries ensure that we do not allow fairness, measurable today at great cost. Hence the reason for the upper, middle and lower classes. This works perfectly in ensuring that we never achieve fairness in any way shape or form. We pay for and listen to people (highly educated) to tell us that we are all making a difference. Whilst I agree people have a little more it is all still relative in terms of inequality since day one of this planet. The rich get richer (and sometimes share), the middle ground pays for it and the poor stay poor.

21. **Man will eventually destroy this world that we live in:** One of Dad's sayings as we grew up. Now it matters not about the context of the word man in the header, it means male or female. Rest assured whether it is in equal terms or not, damage to the way we live is constant. For all that has been learnt since day one of this life, no one has ever stopped to think about evolution (except Darwin) in the true sense and what exactly it means. More importantly how do we as a human race sustain it? Problem now of course is that each country on this planet has a different agenda, simply put this means the world as we know it will become catastrophic. The only thing we do not know is the speed of progress. Don't get me wrong people have questioned evolution and the damage we are doing. But not until the established way that we as human beings live was already way out of control. It is everyone's

fault; leaders could not change it if they tried. The way markets are driven ensures that destruction on a massive scale is ensured. Differences of the people on our planet also ensure it will happen. We were given a chance at the birth of human life and we simply blew it. No matter what words I use now it is no longer a matter of if, but when. Scholars of yesteryear warned against it and scholars of today warn against it. We are today listening but it's too late (or is it? Always have to have a get out clause!). People throughout the ages as we know will say that they only played with the cards they were dealt with. As far as we know it is down to the **MEN,** who wanted to be the strongest on the planet, from yesteryear that started this mess. If we had put women in charge I would dare to suggest that the world would be much more peaceful now than it is. Who or what allowed **MEN** to become the strongest must be rueful of our progress through life. Before someone points out the obvious I know that some women were also notorious but on nowhere near the same scale as **MEN**.

22. **Is the story of God and Jesus the best story ever told?**

23. **<u>Aging:</u>** We all know that each day of our lives we get older and age accordingly, some better than others. Lifestyles that we lead have an impact on the aging process. It suddenly struck me that we as human beings seem to live our lives in similar fashion, and the ages below are only rough guidelines and could change either way i.e. or e.g.:

- From birth to our teenage years we want to be older than we actually are

- From our teenage years to thirty plus we are absolutely invincible, not a care in the world, oblivious to everything and anything
- From thirty plus to death we live in reverse and want to be younger again

24. **<u>Statistics</u>:** Definition of given word = **TRUTHFUL LIES** written by myself in 2008. Note: In a book called Eclipse or Empire written by H.B.Gray & Samuel Turner on page 2 "Statistics have always had an evil reputation. They have been branded as a superlative form of lies" it does go on and even quotes Churchill himself as disliking stats! This was written in 1916.

25. **<u>Melancholy:</u>** So what exactly is it? Suffice to say that intermittently throughout our lives we all, and I mean all, suffer from it without realising it. It was talked about many years ago (300+) by eminent people of society back in the days of Pepys, James Boswell, Dr Johnson and Robert Burton (Author). They understood it occurred, not always why but knew that when it did they were incapacitated for as long as it took them to snap out of it. That, I am afraid is very much the way to deal with it, simply by snapping out of it. The difficult bit is understanding when it is happening. Yet it blights our life as much today as it did back then. To think that we live in a more developed society, yet our forbears understood and acted upon it much better than we do. It seems all to be about a feeling of restlessness, downturn in luck, mild depression, etc. If we all self-analysed more perhaps we could cope with life on life's terms much more easily. So my polite suggestion would be to read up about the true definition of melancholy, once understood deal with it as it occurs

and live a wonderful and much more appreciative life (GOOD LUCK).

26. **Modern Technology/World:** Who or whatever created this world gave society an evolutionary scale. Reading any piece of interpretive history it seems that evolvement was very slow to begin with. But during the last 200 years the pace of growth has taken off faster than any jet plane ever could. It has become so fast that we barely remember what happened yesterday. Onward to tomorrow never looking back, how sad that we are losing some of our means of interaction.

27. **Autobiography** and not **Biography**, simple really. Write the story yourself and not have it written by another, immaterial of some of the stories that we read which are great but also are a dictum of **No 3.**

28. **Reality versus Expectation:** Well we cannot all become Prime Minister or indeed King or Queen. Some people are simply happy with who they are, others strive to be different. Life then switches from peace to constant growth. The ability within each soul to accept just the way they are is too often questioned. Questioned by each other, the media and so called professionals which seems to end in disharmony. Now to explain a little, the world needs workers, people who are just happy to do no more than provide. If we accepted this more and didn't breed false expectation at all levels harmony would take over. We all want to be better (or do we?), this creates disharmony as previously stated. I can hear you all now saying is this guy for real? Simply by thinking that you have subscribed to all of the above! The reality is we do not have enough jobs available to allow everyone to work.

Or do we? That in itself breeds inequality, class divide and scorn. I'm not for one minute saying that we should all change and give up our lifestyles. However to create reality and expectation we require change, both of thought and actuality. In order to create an all out work ethic, we must ensure that all on benefits work for the money. Again I can hear you ask 'why should they work?' Well ask them to carry out roles that in turn allow us all to benefit and reduce our outgoings. Things such as, refuse collection (reduce Council Tax), provide the vehicles and in turn proof of effort whilst not fully employed. They in turn keep the benefits they are living on, build self esteem and have a proven record of intent for future employers. I could list quite a few more but refuse to upset your intelligence. So now you see that reality and expectation in itself could reduce many issues within our society.

29. **Houses:** At the age of 19 I lived in my own council house for 1 year this was in 1979. Thereafter I did not share a house with a partner again until 1989, this was in Army quarters. We lived in Germany until 1994, then moved to London to further Army quarters from 1994-1996. Then to another Army quarter from 1996-2000. Then at the grand age of 39 we bought our first home in Sherburn in Elmet. We never moved in together as we split up, it was sold in 2002. I bought another house in Nuneaton jointly with my sister and moved in on my own. I was forced into buying her out at a profit for her and lived there until I met my future wife. Marion lived with me until we bought our first home together, a new build in Nuneaton. It was a lovely starter home but we had decided that within the next few years we would move. That sadly was brought forward by having the dreaded neighbours from hell. We then decided if we could afford we'd buy a

detached house. Now we live in a four bed detached in Rugby complete with garage, huge garden and bigger kitchen. We have been here now for five years since the house was built, we grow our own vegetables which we share with our very wonderful neighbours. We even have our own social group just in our street. Not quite sure why I put this in the miscellaneous thoughts chapter. Anyway it's my book so I suppose it does not matter.

When I was growing up in our council house I was unaware there was a stigma attached (rightly or wrongly) to people like us. Even to this day it seems there is a social stigma, for some people, to living in a council house. Equally, as previously stated, I was in awe of people who owned their own house, not realising that at times they were struggling just as much as we were (hope that was reciprocal). Also I thought that all private houses were bigger than ours, at least that's how it seemed in my head. Of course what was really happening here is that I was growing up and still building my educative processes. Now by the time I understood that largely there are no differences (I can hear you all howling at that statement, believing that all rough people come from council estates, let me assure you it is in almost equal measure whether council or private) I looked at the houses I adored as a youngster and thought now that I can afford to buy one I would not. Oh how the mind changes and develops, if only teachers understood that (during my time at school I may add). I feel sure that they are nice houses, what has changed is myself, not them. Anyway we are all doing the best that we can within the means that we each possess, if only people did not aim too high in case of falling back down. Temptation eh, we can afford it, or can we?

30. As I **journey through life** it seems funny now that I am past the invincible stage but I treasure my memories. Questions are often raised within my head, some I can answer but with others I struggle to comprehend the meaning to things that I once thought I knew. Other than my beautiful wife I don't really think I have a friend in this world, one rather hopes that I am wrong in this summation. Perhaps I have them but do not know it. Dr Johnson gives his definition of a friend as "One joined to another in mutual benevolence and intimacy" (**My WIFE**). He goes on in fact to list no less than eight explanations of the word friend. For sure at some stages through life I have met and enjoyed limited friendships. I wonder what it is that I am envious of in the quest to understand what a friend is. It might be likely that it is me who is at fault in both understanding and the wanting of one. I have my family but even they seem distant, that also includes my daughter. Do I have it and not know or see it, although I love company I am in essence a private person. Now I am searching for reasons as opposed to excuses, which I hate when people make them. We have become a society embedded in making excuses; this can also affect a friendship.

Why do my family not wish to spend time together as once we used to? It appears that all that our parents taught us has been pushed to one side. I know we are all different but the simple things in life should be shared. Do they not realise that I'm interested in each of their lives? Equally I would like to share mine with them, family get together, holidays and visits. Mum and Dad would be turning in their graves that in so short a time, since they both left us, we have become parted. All it simply requires is effort.

31. **Friendship:** In an earlier part of this book I intimated that I felt devoid of friendship (other than my Wife). If you were careful you may have spotted that I also intimated that the fault or feeling lay at my door. Indeed I may have it in abundance at varying times but do not ordinarily notice it. That said in order to gain an independent view I asked a very good friend to write down his thoughts on friendship. Please read the following and more importantly do not stop at the sentence end!. Allow your minds to go further and seek full meaning from each paragraph. They cover a multitude of scenarios;

Friendship is troublesome and shouldn't be. For men, certainly, it's always a risk. For women, I don't know; it can seem as if it's safer, it can seem frightening too.

How safe is intimacy with another? Not very.

So we bluster and engage in rituals, we act and pretend. With age we mellow, but become more distant. Friendship may not be so easy, it seems.

When we first have the opportunity to act adult, our friends are our fellow performers. We audition one another, and try out roles, test our limits together and experience intense intimacy.

But somehow this gets scarier and scarier. New friendships don't come quite so easily, and old ones begin to feel dated. We look back on friendships with nostalgia, just as we look back on the 60s or the 70s or the 80s. And there is a hint of embarrassment that we really could have behaved like that, just as much as we wore overlarge flared trousers, overtight shirts, and overdeveloped collars and ties.

But we don't get over the best of friendships. Somehow they stay alive despite the years, despite the distance and the time between our meetings. True friends are always with us, and we grow together. We don't play roles, but we find ourselves in the mirror of the other. And as we age, we age together; even when apart.

The strangest feeling is the gasp of recognition when the friend from decades ago, returns to embrace you; the weight may have gone, or more likely arrived, the hair may have gone or become the strangest shade, the height, teeth, eyes, hands are not quite the same, but friendship remains. Instantly, and intimately.

For every true friendship, however, there are many which remain one-act plays. Or soliloquys. Or a period piece. Such that on review, we laugh as much at our lack of taste, snigger at our gaucheness, and pity our younger selves.

So we should. We should care for our histories, and our friendships. There is no shame in the lives we lead, whether solitary or embedded with friends. We should try to work through the trouble, take the risk, abandon safety and embrace intimacy, and warmly welcome the rich pattern of our lives. Let us try to abandon the pretence, and the acting, and find ourselves as children and adults.

Our friends are our opportunity to do just that. By nurturing our friendships, we love and respect ourselves.

(Alan Taylor, 16 September 2012)

Please read, read again, read again, and with a bit of luck you/we will find from it all we need to know about friendship and its many meanings. (Thank you Alan)

Chapter XI

FUTURE

I suppose I ought to leave this chapter blank, after all the future is not yet here. Would anyone understand if I left it blank? For sure the educated amongst you probably would. The question is should we even write at all on something that is not here and subject to change daily? Well let me remind you Nostradamus did!

The easy ones are as follows what do I, or any one of us want from the future:

- Peace and absolute harmony between countries and each other
- Religious harmony and not division, differences kept private
- Don't go back in history but go forward
- Happy and healthy lives
- Family values to be sustained (return in some cases)
- Neighbourly harmony
- No wars or genocide
- Less tax, stagnation of collections for a few years so pay increases can actually take effect in each household
- To see and speak to our parents again
- Enjoy work and not see it as a chore
- Total equality, not of education but in living (working for it wherever and whenever possible)
- Stop the think tanks dreaming up impossible schemes (go back to basics)

- Take a lesson from history as we know it and lighten the load for the middle income earner. The rich can afford to get round most of it and yes I appreciate that, they do pay tax. Most of us however cannot afford to employ our very own accountant to get us out of paying tax
- Sustain profit without growth = less greed
- Balance the world's population to the planet's capabilities

For myself I seek the total love from my present wife as I will give and can assure her of mine in return. The energy to provide us with a happy life until the day we die. We seek to meet and share our life with as many different people as we can, massively including family on both sides. It would be my dearest wish to have a relationship with my daughter and her daughter without judgement. I sincerely hope it is not too late.

To see all our nephews and nieces grow up into well balanced people and to learn from them as their world constantly changes and evolves.

To be courteous to as many members of this world as I can be, especially my neighbours. We seem on that aspect alone to be losing that very essential skill and all of us are slipping into our very own worlds.

A realisation of good old fashioned values not measured against false expectation, the young today deem it their right to have all that we understood we had to work for. Without understanding that you cannot have things if you cannot afford them, unfortunately media and advertising would have you believe otherwise. The knock on effect of this is encouraged by each successive government, who then seek to introduce strategies to make it introducibly (not a word, but I made it up and it's my book) acceptable.

"Life is best understood backwards, but it must be lived forwards"

We live, we learn, the question is "do we utilise everything that we have learned to the full or have we become selective as to our own needs?"

I'm rather glad and equally disappointed that I will not be here in a few hundred years from now. Saddened by what we think we know as a world and what little we are doing to put it right. The future for whoever may be reading this is probably life in a huge sky soaring tower in a single square room. In this room is everything required at the touch of a switch (kitchen, bedroom etc.). Things such as countryside will no longer exist, pushed aside to build upon, memories of it shown weekly on the local blog or TV or whatever medium is in place. Food will be a genetically processed tablet, the more money you have buys a better tablet which in turn equates to your own social standing. In a nutshell no better off than where we are today, poor people still poor and rich people still rich, paid for by middle ground society. Unless governments are brave enough to curb population growth, planet earth is well on its way to total destruction and or Armageddon. In this world only the strong do survive which shows that we have actually learned nothing throughout generations of life so far.

Now let's think about the above thought provoking paragraph, in essence autocracy will need to rule the way we live for a while. Tough decisions need to be made, back to one child per couple, let people actually shrink the world's population and utilise all existing buildings and build no more unless on existing sites. **GOOD LUCK** to society, because life is actually a wonderful thing. Live and enjoy and please do be part of the whole process that makes life worth living not just for you but for others as well. It truly is a wonderful planet, its provision thought out carefully by whoever created it. Society needs to take its foot off the gas a bit and live life in equal measure. This means all members of the planet including animals. Get rid of poverty. Banish any country from being the strongest, sadly the downside is that criminals i.e. murderers should themselves be killed. Create equal wealth for all and not just the chosen, many people reading this will probably think is he dreaming of the perfect world. I do so wish it were fair, but it is not, unless we search deep and make the changes necessary.

I will be sad to leave this world when my time eventually comes; frustrating as life is at times the excitement of living makes you want it to last forever. I love the constant evolvement of ideas, the changing ways and the recognition to accept and deal with it. As we get older we become a little cynical, often forgetting that we ourselves were once young and lived with great gusto. Never thinking that we would one day age, funny thing is when you're young you wish to be older and when you're older you wish to be younger. I would like to say that so far I've got everything right throughout my life, but that would be a lie. Constantly searching for answers and being analytical, it has to be said that I have got the vast majority of it right. Obviously through reading this book there are things that still remain (in the future) to resolve. One day whether it appears in this book or not I hope to have all the missing factors in place. People seek comfort through many mediums, and once recognised they use them often. They can be a loving partner, curling up in bed alone or dreaming. We will call them trigger points, once established as a part of your life, and used as often as needed, your life will become richer. I hope I'm not lecturing people.

In life we are taught many things, we learn from a whole array of processes. I mentioned a book earlier in this one called 'How to Be Happy Though Human'. Within this book it tries to make us understand how to live life simply, but therein lies the problem. What we should, as human beings, practice without question is how to live life simply without negative complications. Here follows sayings that were shared with me from my parents and/or from reading books (history) and should continue into the FUTURE;

- **Keep it simple**
- **Never let an excuse be the reason why you don't do it**
- **Live every day as though its your last**
- **There is beauty in everyone**
- **Diversity is the spice of life**
- **Every day is a good day if you wake up alive (my Dad's favourite saying)**
- **Hello my beauty (the absolute best greeting for a loved one or very good friend)**
- **If you do not love yourself how can you love another?**
- **Love does not always have to be equal**
- **Share**
- **No such word as can't**

HISTORY RESPECTS NOTHING

www.ingramcontent.com/pod-product-compliance
Lightning Source LLC
Chambersburg PA
CBHW062057080426
42734CB00012B/2680